Living With A Phenomenal Memory

Living With A Phenomenal Memory

◆

How an Ordinary Man Developed Amazing Memorization Skills

Frank Healy

iUniverse, Inc.
New York Lincoln Shanghai

Living With A Phenomenal Memory
How an Ordinary Man Developed Amazing Memorization Skills

iUniverse books may be ordered through booksellers or by contacting:

iUniverse
2021 Pine Lake Road, Suite 100
Lincoln, NE 68512
www.iuniverse.com
1-800-Authors (1-800-288-4677)

ISBN: 978-0-595-45095-4 (pbk)
ISBN: 978-0-595-69441-9 (cloth)
ISBN: 978-0-595-89406-2 (ebk)

Printed in the United States of America

To my parents, brother, sister, and extended family
You always accepted and nourished my uniqueness

Contents

Preface

When I was five years old I memorized an entire year of the calendar in a few days. Over the next few years I memorized several hundred years worth of dates, daily weather facts, daily news, and scores of additional information with minimal effort. I now know which day of the week every date occurs from 1752 to 2999. I know daily weather in the Philadelphia area since 1966. I know tons of facts about the Beatles, Marx Brothers, the History of Space Flight, and a plethora of additional subjects. This book is an autobiography of what life was like having this phenomenal memory.

My goal in writing this was to delve into the mental processes I used to memorize the information, and to convey to you, the reader the thinking in a clear and concise way as if you were memorizing the information yourself. The secondary goal is to provide you with some amusing stories about what it was like having a phenomenal memory and being an ordinary person otherwise.

Many people who have memorized the calendar or other facts to an extraordinary degree are autistic savants. This means that they are extraordinary in their area of expertise but severely deficient in other areas. Specifically, they lack the ability to excel in social situations and to empathize with others. Some of them also have mental retardation; therefore they would not have the ability to articulate how they memorize. Since I am not autistic, and I am a Licensed Professional Counselor with a Masters in Counseling Psychology, I have the ability to understand my own mental processes, and articulate them in a book. This book is the culmination of a two-year study on how I memorize the information.

For those of you who are enamored with titles, I will say that I have never competed in the United States, or World Memory Championships, so I am not officially a grandmaster. I am more interested in making a study of the methods I use to develop my skills. My greatest hope is that by exposing to the world how I developed my memory a contribution can be made to the fields of education and psychology, and many people will be helped to develop their own capacities. Furthermore, most people do not have a dire need to look at 100 faces and immediately memorize the names of the people who have them, or memorize 100 words in a list. However, students need to memorize information, and people need to memorize information for their work. So this book is designed to help people in their everyday concerns.

Introduction

Living With a Phenomenal Memory is an all around testimony on my life experience of having a memory developed to a level beyond the level that most people attain. Some chapters focus solely on the thoughts I had, and the mental processes that led to good memory skills. Perhaps unwittingly, I used some processes of Boolean algebra as well as mnemonics to memorize before I had a formal understanding of the names of the processes. Years later, when I read books and listened to tapes on the subject of memory improvement, it was a struggle to apply their techniques, since I had already created my own methods. Essentially I used my imagination and employed anything that was helpful. Some chapters detail how I memorized specific information for my own entertainment, and others detail how I memorized things for practical use. It is recommended that you read each chapter a few times until you understand the principles. Other chapters detail how I developed my skills in different stages of my life. Hopefully these chapters will, provide some entertainment to you, the reader. Some chapters include puzzles for your enjoyment. Finally, several end with a section entitled What You Can Do. It includes tips for developing your own skills if you are interested.

Through my own experiences of teaching memory skills, I have found that there are as many things that people struggle to memorize, as there are people. Therefore, it is not possible to include every exercise that people might need for their use. I have given some examples of exercises that people will need for their use, such as schoolwork, and I have given some general tips throughout the text. The final chapter is exercises you can use to improve your memory with an entertaining birthday exercise that can help you memorize anything numerical. I have found that most general exercises can be used in a variety of circumstances to fit a variety of needs. Please see the afterword for a way to get your specific questions answered.

1

A Five Year Old Prodigy

I first realized I had extraordinary memory skills when I was five and a half years old. I was home sick from school for a week, and my uncle had given me a calendar for the year 1966. Feeling too ill to be up playing with toys I lay in bed staring at the calendar and felt fascinated by it. Soon I began noticing patterns. If I knew the day of the week of every day from the first week you could calculate the rest of the month by adding 7's. For example, if the first day of the month was a Saturday you could calculate 1, 8, 15, 22, and 29 to get the subsequent Saturdays in the month. I quickly found it easy to use rote memory and just say over and over the sequences.

1	2	3	4	5	6	7
8	9	10	11	12	13	14
15	16	17	18	19	20	21
22	23	24	25	26	27	28
29	30	31				

I would say in my head several times, One, eight, fifteen, twenty-two, twenty-nine, and do the same with all of the sequences. Now I was able to tell any date in a month as long as I knew the first seven. For example, if I wanted to know the twenty-first day of a month I would just know when the seventh was because it is in that sequence. So if the seventh was on a Saturday I could quickly figure out seven, fourteen, twenty-one, so the 21st would be on a Saturday.

I expanded my skills further by using more elaborative rehearsal. Elaborative rehearsal is where you make a connection of two facts, where there is no obvious connection. This is different from rote rehearsal. In rote rehearsal you say the information over and over again. Many students do this when they are studying, they will take information they need to memorize and say it enough times that they hope it will stick. Imagine that you had an assignment to learn the first ten presidents. You start using rote rehearsal by saying George Washington, John Adams, Thomas Jefferson, James Madison, and James Monroe. So you repeat those names 100 times. Then you repeat the next five 100 times, John Quincy Adams, Andrew Jackson, Martin Van Buren, William Henry Harrison, and John Tyler. Then you repeat James Monroe, John Quincy Adams 100 times to bridge the gap. So then you try to say all 10. It sounds like drudgery. Unfortunately many students use rote rehearsal to memorize everything. Conversely, you could use elaborative rehearsal to memorize the same list by doing the following. Think of the bust of George Washington, then imagine it yelling at the Continental Congress and reshaping its head to look like John Adams in the movie 1776. Then you imagine the scene where the committee is meeting and John hands Thomas the quill pen and drafts him to write the Declaration of Independence. Then imagine Thomas Jefferson taking a break from his writing to eat some Dolly Madison ice cream, so now you know that the sequence is Washington the general, Adams the determined and tactless leader of the cause for independence, Thomas Jefferson the writer of the Declaration, and James Madison, the husband of the ice cream queen. Then you imagine when you eat the ice cream you get a real good feeling. Which, if you know some history James Monroe was the president during the Era of Good Feeling. Good feelings don't always last. Soon we had another tactless Adams in the White house, John Quincy Adams. With his fiery Adams tongue another war breaks out. So the next president is former general Andrew Jackson. During the battle one soldier has a fan (van) instead of a gun. Then a bullet rips through the fan and it gets torn. Van Buren is the next president. Nevertheless the fan becomes a bill and it flies up in the air towards the sun, and the sun is narrowing. The next president is William (Bill) Harrison (narrow sun) Finally, the narrow sun falls down into a house and sits on the john, and the john has arms coming out and is laying piles (you decide what) on the floor, John Tyler (piler).

This use of elaborative rehearsal might seem bizarre for someone who is not used to using it. However, if you use your imagination you can learn information much faster than the monotonous repetition and drudgery of rote rehearsal. If I had used rote rehearsal to memorize the calendars I could not have taken my range nearly as far as I did. If I had to sit there and repeat March 1, 1966 Tuesday over again I would have become bored and quit quickly. So here is how I used elaborative rehearsal. I had a favorite television program for every night of the week, what six years old does not? I began glancing at the calendar squares with a quick glance at the month first. Then I would repeat the date in my head a few times—then quietly sing the theme song for my program for that night.

Example: Wednesday October 5—Batman, Batman, Batman.

Saturday December 3—They call him Flipper, Flipper.

The year was 1966—so the prime time T.V. lineup was as follows.

Sunday—Disney. Monday—The Monkees, Tuesday—Combat, Wednesday and Thursday—Batman. Friday—The Green Hornet. Saturday—Flipper.

By making the association of the T.V. show, it's theme, and the calendar date I was able to memorize the entire year in a couple of days. One question you might have is that I might have confused some Wednesdays and Thursdays because Batman was on both days. I circumvented this by picturing Batman with the Wednesdays, and Robin with the Thursdays. Therefore I used both auditory (the songs) and visual (the pictures) cues to make the associations.

What prompted me to memorize the calendar in the first place? I was fascinated by the activity we did in Kindergarten each day. Every morning we would gather in front of a large calendar for the month made of construction paper. The teacher would lead us in a rhythmic chant where we all recited the date. For example, It's Wednesday, September, numeral Twenty Two, Nineteen Sixty Five. I remember when the color of the poster board changed it meant we were in a new month. I also remember observing that after the Christmas break the number was different at the top of the calendar. I was inwardly laughing when we did the usual chant and most students said it was 1965 instead of 1966.

One afternoon I was in the backyard thinking about the calendar activity. I began to recite the months in my head. This had not been given as a class assignment, I just had the natural inclination to do it.

Now I had memorized an entire year in a couple of days. I recovered from my illness and resumed my life as a child and a scholar. I began making mental notes throughout each day about events that were occurring in my life. Five to ten times each day I would notice what was happening and make a mental note of which day it was happening on. For example—Monday August 1—we went on our vacation to the shore. Friday September 30—We moved to a new house. I remembered something from each date, not just the ones where something significant happened, but everyday events such as things that happened at school.

In addition to events I also took notice of the weather every day, I noticed if it was sunny, rainy, snow, warm, or cold. Now I know the daily Philadelphia area whether every day for the past 41 years.

As 1966 ended I realized that my range of dates I knew was ending so I began memorizing the New Year. This was easier because I quickly discovered a pattern. Each date moved over one place from the previous year so all I had to do was take the 1966 date and go forward one. For example, we noted that December 3 was on a Saturday so the next year it would be a Sunday. I quickly doubled my range. I continued to note the weather, personal events, and significant news events for each date.

The following year, 1968 was a leap year. I quickly figured out why they call it a leap year. After February 29 the dates skip a day. Let's go back to the December 3 example. 1966—Saturday, 1967—Sunday, 1968 Tuesday. It skips the Monday because of the leap. This skip continues through the first two months of the following year. We can look at a more recent example, January 1, 2004 was a Thursday, but January 1, 2005 was a Saturday because there was a February 29 in between.

As the years went by I noted each day, the day of the week, the weather, personal experiences, and whether there were any significant news events that day. They say that the more you connect new information to old information the more likely the new information will be retained. The more years went by the more I connected different things together. I would connect events and weather with previous events for that day.

Example—Thursday June 1, 1972—sunny and seasonal. I was on a camping trip. I remember all of us gathering around the campfire singing songs, such as "There were three Jolly fishermen, they should have gone to Amster shh, we're going to say that naughty word, they should have gone to Amsterdam". It is amazing how easily one is entertained at age 12. Tuesday June 1, 1971 my first Boy Scout meeting, it was also sunny and seasonal. At the end of the meeting one of the scouts came in his baseball uniform and said my team won, they beat his team. Monday June 1, 1970—Sunny and seasonal—Learning how to cast a fishing rod. Sunday June 1, 1969 sunny and seasonal—Getting a new diesel for our model train set. Saturday June 1, 1968—sunny and cold after a few days of unseasonably warm weather. Getting angry with my parents because they said it was too cold to go to the pool. Thursday June 1, 1967—Sunny and cold after a record breaking cold May. We went on a class field trip to a bakery. It was also the day the Beatles released Sergeant Pepper's Lonely Hearts Club Band. I have a similar list for all dates for the past 41 years.

I categorized all 7 possibilities that a date could fall on. I decided to categorize them from March 1 to February 28 into septets. Each year February 28 falls on the same day of the week that March 1 fell the previous year. There are actually 52 weeks and one day in a year. For example, 2007 begins and ends on a Monday, which makes it 52 weeks and one day. In a leap year there are 52 weeks and two days. So 2008 will begin on a Tuesday and end on a Wednesday. Since counting a year from January 1 to

December 31 would mean there are 14 possibilities for a year to be. Years ago the telephone book designated calendars 1 through 14. Calendars one through seven would be the common (non leap years) which began (January 1 on Sunday through Saturday) Calendars eight through 14 would be the leap years beginning Sunday through Saturday as follows.

Common years

1. January 1 on Sunday 1995, 2006

2. January 1 on Monday 2001, 2007

3. January 1 on Tuesday 1991, 2002

4. January 1 on Wednesday 1997, 2003

5. January 1 on Thursday 1998, 2009

6. January 1 on Friday 1999, 2010

7. January 1 on Saturday 2005, 2011.

Leap years

1. January 1 on Sunday. 1984, 2012

2. January 1 on Monday 1996, 2024

3. January 1 on Tuesday 1980, 2008

4. January 1 on Wednesday 1992, 2020

5. January 1 on Thursday 2004, 2032

6. January 1 on Friday 1988, 2016

7. January 1 on Saturday 2000,2028.

To designate every year with 14 possibilities seemed complicated even for someone of my abilities. So I devised what seemed to me to be an easier way to designate the dates. I decided to designate seven septets which begin on March 1 and end on the following February 28. This system would work so each septet began and ended with the same day of the week, so each septet would have 53 instead of 52 of a particular day of the week. I designated them

1st—53 Sundays
2nd—53 Saturdays
3rd—53 Fridays
4th—53 Thursdays
5th—53 Wednesdays
6th—53 Tuesdays
7th—53 Mondays

It might appear to be easier to just designate it by the position of the days of the week. The 1st would still have the two Sundays, 2nd two Mondays etc. but I noticed certain events happen where the earliest is on the 1st an the latest is on the 7th. For example, the earliest Easter can fall on is March 22 which would put it in the first when March 22 is a Sunday. (It has not fallen on March 22 since 1818) the latest Easter date is April 25, which would be in the 7th for April 25 to be a Sunday. It fell in April 25 in1943 and will fall on the 25th again in 2038. I designated the typical school year similarly. In a non leap year the date of Labor Day shows what calendar will begin six months later. In 2006 Labor Day was September 4th and March 1, 2007 began the 4th. Here is the designation for the last few and the next few years.

7th—Monday March 1, 2004 to Monday February 28, 2005.
6th—Tuesday March 1, 2005 to Tuesday February 28, 2006.
5th—Wednesday March 1, 2006 to Wednesday February 28, 2007.
4th—Thursday March 1, 2007 to Thursday February 28, 2008.
Friday February 29, 2008—Skip the 3rd.
2nd—Saturday March 1, 2008 to Saturday February 28, 2009.
1st—Sunday March 1, 2009 to Sunday February 28, 2010.
7th—Monday March 1, 2010 to Monday February 28, 2011.

6th—Tuesday March 1, 2011 to Tuesday February 28, 2012.
Wednesday February 29, 2012 skip the 5th.

I further discovered that the day of the week that February 29 falls on is the same day that the septet that is being skipped has 53 of. For example, Friday February 29 skips the 3rd and the 3rd has 53 Fridays in it, and Wednesday February 29 skips the 5th and the 5th has two Wednesdays in it. This pattern follows for all February 29ths.

Using this formula I created I was able to attach a number from 1 to 7 on any year, and then know the entire year. So in just two more days I knew every date in the Gregorian calendar. I also figured the mathematical logic that:

A.   If there are only seven possibilities for a date to fall on, and

B.   The leap occurs every four years then

C.   The calendars must repeat themselves every 4x7 or 28 years.

Obviously different sets of dates repeat more frequently than every 28 years, however, they always repeat every 28 years. Otherwise they go in sequences of five, six, or eleven years.

Example: the 7th—1976, 1982, 1993, 1999, 2004 and 2010

But 1982, 1993, and 1999 were not leap years, so January and February of those years were 1st's with February 28 on a Sunday. In 1976 and 2004 January and February were the 2nd, with February 28 on a Saturday and February 29 on the Sunday. Go to any year and it will be the same as 28 years before or later. Discovering this allowed me to memorize the more distant years by associating them to a closer year. The only exception to the 28-year rule was that three out of four century changes skip the leap. For example, 2000 was a leap year, 1700, 1800, and 1900 were not. So three out of four century change years you don't skip the date for a year and you have eight years between leaps. For example, May 21 1899 was a Sunday. Then you have February 28, 1900 a Wednesday, no February 29 so you go from the 5th to the 4th septet, instead of skipping to the 3rd. Then March 1, 1900 was a Thursday and May 21, 1900 was a Monday. So it went just one day from Sunday to Monday. Let's compare the millennium change, where 2000 was a leap year. May 21, 1999 was a Friday, in the 7th septet. Then February 28, 2000 was a Monday. There was a February 29, Tuesday, which caused a skip of the 6th septet. Wednesday March 1 began the 5th septet, and May 21 was a Sunday, not a Saturday. This leap in 2000 when, shall we say we leaped the leap on the last three-century changes caused some of the consternation over the possibility of Y2K. This glitch in the system could have caused computers to be off one day starting on March 1, 2000. So we weren't out of the woods yet on January 1, 2000.

I remember as far back as the late 1980's there was concern About Y2K. On the evening of Saturday May 9, 1987 I was at an Astronomy Day talk when the president of our club, a highly knowledgeable and respected astronomer and computer programmer quoted some misinformation. He said that every fourth turn of the century they skip the leap year but they have it on the other three, so that would throw the computers off on March 1, 2000. I remember attempting to correct him in front of everybody and his annoyance over it. I now realize that it was a rather boorish thing to do.

What was next? Now that I had the entire calendar memorized as far as it could go what else was there? As I mentioned previously I was memorizing the weather each day, so I became interested in weather trends. I found it interesting that one winter we would have no snow and another year there would be snow on the ground continuously from New Years until Easter.

My interest in weather trends began in 1973. That winter we had no measurable snow in the Philadelphia area the entire winter. That was the first time that had happened since we kept records. Than I noticed that Easter was very late, April 22, so the combination of mild winter and late Easter caused everything to be in summer like condition by Easter. All the leaves had fully sprouted and all the flowers were out. This was not a usual occurrence.

In subsequent years I would memorize anything that interested me. I memorized facts about the Beatles, including the dates of all their album releases and personal events during their six years of fame. Similarly I memorized facts about the Marx Brothers, the history of space flight, Asian astrology, and many other facts. The more facts I knew the easier it became to attach new information to old, since there was more old information. Now I can make many associations with any date.

Example: July 10, 1979 Tuesday—in 4th septet—the Asian year of the ram—Other July 10 Tuesdays include 1973, 1984, 1990, 2001, and 2007. The weather that day was sunny and seasonal. We had a brand new pool in the backyard. The Pan American Games were being played in San Juan. Some people were afraid to go outside because the Skylab was falling, it would land in an Australian farm field on the 12th. The following weekend I went on a mini vacation to New York City with my family. That evening I went to see the Philadelphia Phillies play. They won the game on a pinch-hit home run by Del Unser, his third in a row, which was a new team record.

Making up stories, which helped me remember the facts and tie everything together, did much for my memorizing. There will be a plethora of examples in subsequent chapters, but for now I will share how I created a story for this particular date. See if you can associate the pictures with the facts.

First, as in 1966 I visualized the calendar date, the ten in the third block in a row. The block now shows a moving picture of a ram walking along. The sun is shining overhead. Suddenly the ram falls into a swimming pool. The pool then becomes the size of an Olympic pool with the lanes marked and the ram is in one lane with several other swimmers competing. There is a sign for the old Pan Am airlines waving above the pool. The spectators in the stands are all Hispanic people. One of them is singing the part of the song "Life Can Be Free In America" the part that goes "I want to go back to San Juan". Suddenly there is a bright light in the sky and a nearby man in farm clothes is preparing to throw a boomerang towards it, he says I am practicing for the 12th, then I will go to New York". As he prepares to practice his boomerang becomes a baseball bat and he is in a Phillies uniform with the name Unser on the back and he is singing Farmer in the Dell as he hits the ball. The umpire pinches him and yells "Homer three" instead of strike three.

Similarly, I would make up stories as I went about my days, so each day that I experienced had a story. For days, which I had not been born yet, I would imagine the situations in history that I read about. And connect them in a similarly entertaining way.

Sometimes I would create my own mental gymnastics. I began looking for things that happened on each septet that seemed exclusive to that septet. The fourth septet produced national and international crises. 1962-63 had the Cuban Missile Crisis. 1973-74 was the Watergate scandal. Even though the break in was Saturday June 17, 1972 (5th) the hearings with John Dean, H.R. Haldeman, John Ehrlichman, John Mitchell, and Alexander Butterworth were during the summer of 1973 (4th) Then the Saturday Night massacre was October 20, 1973 where Archibald Cox, Elliott Richardson, and John Ruckehouse were fired. The "I am not a Crook" speech was on Saturday November 17, 1973 and in January of 1974 those of us who were alive were going to work and school in the dark because Daylight Savings Time was moved to January.

The next fourth occurred in 1979–1980. The summer of 1979 saw an oil shortage where people spent hours at a time in gas lines. Then on Sunday November 4 The Ayatollah Khomeni took U.S. hostages. In 1984—85 we were lucky to not have a crisis. America beamed with pride as the economy was getting better and we hosted the Olympics in Los Angeles, albeit sans Soviet Union and the Eastern bloc. The next 4th 1990-91 was when Saddam Hussein invaded Kuwait on Friday August 3. We then had five and a half months of Desert Shield until Wednesday January 16, 1991 when the air raid on Baghdad began. Then the ground war began on Saturday February 23. The surrender was on Wednesday February 27 just in time to move out of the 4th and into the 3rd.

In the 1996 leap year we skipped the 4th. So the next 4th was in 2001-2002 the year of 9/11. I realize that this is nothing to joke about but I find it interesting that most of the major world crises seem to occur when the calendar is in a particular way.

Being a Philadelphia sports fan (no, I will not be extolling the virtue of patience) I noticed how teams fared in particular septets. Every time we are in the 5th the Eagles start winning again after having a losing season the previous year. In 1978 it was Dick Vermiel's first winning season, in 1995 Ray Rhodes took the team to 10-6 after 7-9 in 94. In 2000 it was Andy Reid's first winning season 11-5 after going 5-11 in 99. And in 2006 they reversed their 6-10 record of 2005 and went 10-6. They had better stay good now because the next 5th is not until 2017.

Essentially I made information interesting by using my imagination. However, I believe anyone can do this with practice. When I create the stories I use not only visual cues, but also I imagine sounds, emotions, and where appropriate touch. For example, with the ram falling into the pool I imagined the sensation of falling into a pool and getting wet, the sound of the splash. The feelings of anger and embarrassment that the ram must have felt, and how funny it looked. Each of those cues made it easier to recall the information. The next few chapters will show how I used my imagination for schoolwork and practical things.

What can you do?

All these facts and figures may seem overwhelming to you if you think you just have average or below average memory ability. However, there are things you can do. If you are not interested in history or weather you could start with a subject you are interested in. If you take the above example of the presidents, and you are more interested in sports, imagine all the men playing baseball, and the less notable presidents strike out and the more notable ones hit home runs. You add this to the examples already given and you will further get the facts in your head and remember them better.

2

The Early Years

Child experts agree that most children cannot remember events in their lives before the age of three. This is called infantile amnesia. The brain in insufficiently developed at that age and they lack the cognitive capacity to decide which things are important enough to remember. Perhaps I had a capacity for memory that was above the average even as a baby. My first memory was singing the song "Moon River" with my mother at the age of 21 months I can vouch that that was when it was because that was when it was a hit by Andy Williams. I also remember waking up on Christmas morning in my blue crib and watching my parents demonstrate how to play with the toys before they took me out. I was aware that my brother was down the hall in his yellow crib.

There are other events that I remember before age three. In our home we frequently had music playing. My father had been a musician in his young years and my parents were fond of bands and musicals. I remember a song we would play "green green, it's really green" and "life is a hard road to travel". I remember singing Life is a Hard Road to Travel at a party. One of my parents friends told them "A two year old philosopher, what will he be like when he is twenty?" Years later, when I was 34 years old I was at a party where they played the same album and I had an instant flashback to that other party 32 years earlier. I could even see in my mind the people and the furniture from that other time.

I remember a birthday party for a child in the neighborhood when I was two. Most two year olds have not mastered the art of sharing toys, and it certainly was not my forte. As children and their parents were filing in with toys for the protagonist (Birthday boy) I remember grabbing on to them and throwing a tantrum when they tried to give it to the correct child.

My brother was born when I was two years and three months old. Although my parents described the event in detail I have no specific recollection of the birth or their coming home from the hospital. Perhaps I was traumatized about not being the only child anymore. So I let infantile amnesia get the best of me on that one. I do remember when my sister was born; I was six and a half years old and had begun memorizing the dates.

So, I do remember many events before age three. Now, as an adult I teach Child Psychology at my local community college. We do an exercise called "Your first memory, how old were you". Usually, about one third of the students claim to remember events before age three. I think that if an event has a strong emotional significance they will remember it.

After age three my memories did become more vivid. I was able to recall everyday events and not just significant events. I remember playing in the yard, swinging on swings. I remember the complete layout of our yard and every yard on the street. Including all the play equipment, trees, fences etc. I remember the bigger boys hanging from the rim of the swing set and walking with their hands from one end to the other. The smaller kids (myself included) could duck under the fences to get from one yard to the other. That was, until my father built a wire fence around our yard. I was about four years old, and I remember my parents talking about putting up a wire fence in not very pleasant tonality. Then, when the fence was erected I felt insulted because somehow I concluded that the fence was there because I had been bad. I was four at the time, pretty profound.

Children do go through a phase called animistic thinking where they attribute human thoughts and emotions to objects. As an intelligent and sensitive child I took animistic thinking to extremes. I would play by making my toy trucks, trains and fire engines have conversations with each other. One time I dropped a toy and imagined it needing to go to the doctors for the injury. As the years went by I remembered the events on every birthday, including birthdays of other family members, every Christmas, and every vacation. This included the weather, and what people received for presents. For my third birthday I received a talking puppet of Cecil the

Seasick Sea serpent. Now, maybe that was a precursor to several apartments I lived in where there were ant problems no matter how well I cleaned. Cecil had the same problem on the cartoon show.

In Kindergarten I was curious to know how everything worked. I have described how I memorized the dates. There was additional knowledge I accrued in Kindergarten. We learned a song about remembering your name, address, and telephone number in case you ever lose your way. So, already being a five-year-old expert on memory, my name address and telephone number was easy. However, I wanted more. There must be a way to test this newfound knowledge. The opportunity came when my father brought my brother and I home some compasses from a vending machine at Howard Johnson's. I remembered that north was the direction of the North Pole where Santa lived. I explained to my brother that we could get dibs on the other children and get to see Santa in May, before anyone else got to him and he ran out of presents. It was Tuesday May 10, 1966 and cold enough to be thinking of Christmas. So we brought out compasses and walked several miles through fields, streams (Where my brother fell flat on his face on the water) fences (Where we both got cut) and a country villa (Where we let a white poodle out of the house). Finally we came to a residential neighborhood and knocked on a door. I recited my name, address, and telephone number. The young lady called our house and a few minutes later our mother arrived in a police car. The entire school and neighborhood were in an uproar, but I had gotten to test my knowledge by losing my way.

3

How I Memorized My Work In Elementary School

Perhaps surprisingly, I never told any of my teachers in elementary school about my special ability. It could have been that I did not consider it relevant for school, or maybe I was afraid they would expect too much from me.

It would seem logical that school would come to me easily. It did whenever I chose to pay attention. I began using my skills to compose little stories that helped me remember information. The stories were pictorial with movement and irony. I figured out on my own that the more unrealistic a story the better potential it had for helping me remember the real information.

In school we had weekly readers with stories and pictures. I recall a time when there was a picture of some small donkeys called burros. The teacher explained to us that burros take all the other animals food so they have to make more. I visualized a giraffe frantically using a can opener to open a can of beans. In the background there was a burro approaching. After opening the can at breakneck speed the giraffe says "I had better wolf this down before Billy Burro comes back" whereupon he pours the beans down his throat. I imagined a lump going down his long neck as the food passes. He then breathes a sigh of relief. Meanwhile, the burro lifts one paw, snaps it's claw like someone snapping their fingers in frustration, since he didn't get the food this time.

Realistically, a giraffe does not eat beans. And burros only take the food of smaller animals. However, creating this unrealistic and humorous picture made me remember that basic fact now 40 years later. As I imagined the relief of the giraffe and the frustration of the burro I felt those feelings. I heard in my head his phrase that he needed to wolf the beans down. Hence, I used visual cues, auditory and feeling cues all combined, the more senses you employ in your picture the more likely you will retain it.

I discovered that I could make these pictures to remember anything. Another time we were learning about the Hovercraft. It is a land and sea vehicle in Europe that transports people. Specifically, we were given an example that you could go from Norway to Germany to Greece without changing transportation. First. I visualized the craft itself hovering over a man who was working with wood (making a craft. Then I pictured it on a map of Scandinavia in Norway, going across the sea to Germany, then to Greece. I already had memorized the maps of Europe and the United States, so it was easy to visualize this vehicle going along a map. Then I imagined me riding it over sea and land. The other passengers included some Vikings, German World War 11 soldiers, and Zeus. Predictably the Vikings disembarked in Norway, the soldiers in Germany, and Zeus in Greece.

Many of my visualizations that I used to master schoolwork involved going to places, either on maps or to places I had seen pictures of, and integrating people and things from every day life into them. As you can see by the burro example I would incorporate pictures of things that do not go together, and create an entire story about them. I also discovered that the stories could be as long as I needed them to be if I had a long list of facts. As long as I made clear pictures, made them bizarre, and created movement in them I could create a long story and remember every detail with clarity. The burro story was easy, and anyone over the age of five might be able to remember that they take food. However, as you advance in school it is necessary to remember a plethora of facts regarding a subject. The remainder of this chapter will detail some of the associations I made.

In third grade we were learning about the Solar System. We needed to know the name of each planet, the order out from the sun, and the names of the satellites (moons) that surrounded them. I took a trip through the solar system in my mind and additionally memorized the average distances from the sun, the lengths of their year in earth days, and the gases they are composed of.

Memorizing their names was no problem, since we had already studied Greek and Roman mythology and the planets are named after the gods they created. First I traveled to Mercury. I visualized a red-hot surface with no clouds (Mercury has no atmosphere). The sun being more than twice the size that it appears on earth, although the sky was dark due to the lack of an atmosphere, so I am breathing through a machine like the astronauts. A young man rushes up to me with Mercurial speed and gives me a message (Mercury was the messenger of the gods). Then I ran around twice making two figure 8's to symbolize that Mercury's year is the equivalent of 88 earth days. Then I imagined my aunt (who was born in '43) stretched out from Mercury to the sun so I would remember that Mercury is about 43 million miles from the sun. Before departing for Venus I put on my winter jacket to go and visit the night side of Mercury. I decided it was much too cold on that side so I need to go to a warmer place like Venus.

As I descend through the clouds into Venus I notice the sun is still bigger than on earth, but it is hard to see it through the massive clouds. I can remove my winter coat since it is now close to 800 degrees here. I pictured a woman standing there (Venus) and she is breathing out a lot of air. (Venus has a lot of Carbon Dioxide in its atmosphere). When it became night I though I can get rid of my shorts and put on jeans. (Venus also has nitrogen in it's atmosphere, night—jean). Next to the blurb of the sun was a kid I knew whose birthday was February 24 and had just turned seven. I put him next to the sun to signify the length of a year on Venus 224.7 earth days (February 24 224 and 7).

Next I imagined a baby in our neighborhood that was born in "67 stretching from Venus to the sun to signify it is 67 million miles from the sun.

Next I had to stop home on earth to remind myself that out planet is third in line. Then I noticed that Generalissimo Francisco Franco was stretched out from the Earth to the sun (He was born in 1893 so I used him to remember that the Earth is 93 million miles from the sun.).

As I left Earth for Mars I noticed an irony as I looked back at earth. The Earth seemed to be moving alternately closer and farther from the sun. When it would move close I noticed snow falling on it and I heard people yelling Happy Belated New Year, it's January 3. Then when it moved it's farthest I saw 4th of July fireworks. This was a reminder that the Earth is actually closest to the sun on January 3 and farthest on July 4. How odd, then I pictured the earth at different slants with the sun coming on it. This was a reminder that in the northern hemisphere is hotter in the summer because of the slant of the sun's rays, despite it being further from the sun.

Now it was on to Mars. I noted that this was a short trip since Mars is physically closer to Earth than any other planet. I noticed the red surface, the smaller Sun, and puddles of water. Then I noticed the boxer Cassius Clay (He had not risen to prominence yet or changed his name to Muhammad Ali) stretching from Mars to the Sun, (He was born in January 1942 and Mars in 142 million miles from the sun). Then I saw a demon in the sky and another creature that looked scared of the demon (Mars' moons are Demos and Phobus, so the demon for demos, and the phobic person for phobus). Speaking of demons, then I saw Beelzebub next to the sun in the sky holding a good luck charm. (The previous June 8 I had starred in a school show where I played Beelzebub, the good luck charm represented the number 7. This reminded me that Mars' year is 687 earth days, Beelzebub, June 8, 68 and the good luck charm for 7. Then I have to leave Mars because a war is breaking out. (Mars is the god of war)

Then I sought refuge from the war on the big planet. I figured the king of the gods (Jupiter or Zeus would provide a safe kingdom). The problem was when I got there I was so heavy that I could not stand up. I had a 1 and a 2 on my chest weighing me down (Jupiter's gravitational field is 12 times Earth's.) Despite my heaviness I noticed that there were some balloons floating off into the sky and air rising up from the water. (Jupiter contains helium and hydrogen. The balloons floating away represented helium to me and the oxygen leaving the water signified that hydrogen would be left). The number 12 then flew off my chest into the air and broke off into some moons encircling the planet (at the time it was believed that Jupiter had 12 moons) One of the moons was in the shape of a map of Europe and another was handing the Europe moon a promissory note. (The moon that looked like Europe was Europa, and the one handing the note was Io, I owe). Another moon looked like Calypso, Callisto. The fourth notable moon had pieces of meat landing on it (Ganemede, it was gaining meat). The sun was smaller in the sky here and next to it I pictured Ronald Reagan, then governor of California holding hands with the baseball great Ty Cobb. (Jupiter's year is 11.86 Earth years. Ronald Reagan was born in 1911 and Ty Cobb was born in 1886). Then I saw four school buildings stretching from Jupiter to the sun, with a graduation cap on one. (Jupiter is 478 million miles from the sun. I was slated to graduate from High School in 1978 so by imagining four schools and one with a graduation cap I remembered four then seven eight).

Now I was tired of being so heavy, and I was curious about something I saw in the sky that had rings around it. So I flew to Saturn. The sun was even smaller there and was often obfuscated by the rings. Suddenly the rings became two figure eights and a half figure 8 which stretched form Saturn to the sun (Saturn is 886 million miles from the sun). Next to the sun on Saturn there was a man I knew who owned a junkyard holding hands with my father's cousin who was in medical school at the time. The junkyard owner was born in 1929 and my father's cousin was born in 1946. Saturn's year is 29.46 Earth years.). I noticed I was almost as heavy on Saturn as I was on Jupiter, damn. Nearby there was a poor person who was sick with pneumonia seated on a chair and leaning down. (Two prominent elements on Saturn are ammonia and acetylene).

Maybe now it was time to complain about Jupiter and Saturn's heaviness. I will go to the person in charge of them, Jupiter's father Uranus. As I flew in I noticed a giant paper, which stretched from Uranus all the way to the sun. It said Paris Peace Treaty 1783. (This Treaty was signed in 1783 and Uranus is 1783 million miles from the sun). When I got there they seemed to have the same problem as in Jupiter with balloons floating away and oxygen leaving water. I thought there must be a method to this. (Uranus has helium, hydrogen, and methane in its atmosphere). Next to the dim sun was former president Harry Truman (He was born in 1884. A year in Uranus is 84 Earth years). I thought how on Uranus you would only get one birthday; one Christmas etc. that is if you even lived to 84. Then at least summer vacation would last 21 years.

After this I decided I needed a vacation to a Neptunian resort, so I went to Neptune, but found it similar to Uranus. The helium, hydrogen, and methane were the same. The nice thing was that there was a lot of money stretching from the planet to the sun. Three sets of ten treasure chests, which said one billion on them. (Neptune is about 30 billion miles from the sun). I thought what a financially successful resort. Next to the sun there was the Beatles dancing around in figure 8's because they have just begun having hit records. (It is January 1964, 164, figure 8's, 88 Neptune's year is 164.88 earth years). On Neptune, I visualized the sun being not much brighter than a star.

For some, this might seem more complicated than just using rote rehearsal. Which would consist of saying the information repeatedly and hope it sticks. Personally, I find it the most useful to combine rote memory with the elaborative rehearsal. If you say the information repeatedly you can hear it in your head when it is presented on a test. However, you would not be able to put it in context. For example, Demos and Phobus repeat those words 50 times and you will remember that Demos and Phobus go together. But if you combine the technique I have outlined you will remember that they are Mars moons. If you just use the imaginative technique you might think Mars' moons are Demon and Phobic, since that is how you imagined them. However, if when you get to the Mars part of the journey you imagine the demon and the phobic, and say Demos and Phobus a few times you will remember easily the Demos and Phobus are Mars' moons.

Due to my fecund imagination, English was one of my best subjects in school. When I would read a story it was easy for me to follow along and visualize everything that was happening. Preschoolers don't have to imagine things when they are being read to because the pictures are already provided. This is actually a grooming of their imaginations for when they are older. If they look at enough pictures and associate them with the words eventually they can crate their own pictures when they start reading themselves. Gradually they learn to make their own pictures and the presence of illustrations in books diminishes. For me, it was no trouble following along a story and imagining what was happening. I would visualize the scene, repeat the words in my head if there was dialogue, and imagine how I would feel being the characters. I would often put myself in the story, which helped me maintain interest. For example, when we were being read the Little House books in First Grade I would imagine that the Ingall's had a son too and I was it. When I read Robinson Crusoe I imagined I was the one surviving on the island I also liked his books because they included the dates that the events happened.

Predictably, when I was learning math in school I associated numbers with dates. When learning the times tables I would make the numbers that were being multiplied into one date, and the answer into another. Six times eight is forty eight became, in addition to the rhyme became June 8 6/8 is April 8 4/8. Then I would think of something that happened the previous June 8 and create a bridge with something that happened last April 8.

I treated history like English. When we would learn about a historical event I would imagine the scene, including the visuals, the sounds, and if appropriate, how people might have felt. Sometimes I put myself in the scene, and connected everything. I remember learning about the Louisiana Purchase. It was a purchase of a huge chunk of land out west, which belonged to France. President Thomas Jefferson made the purchase on Monday April 11, 1803 two days before his 60th birthday. Senator Daniel Webster had made a caustic speech opposing the purchase, claiming that it is worthless land. I imagined Daniel Webster feeling angry and passionate making his speech. Thomas Jefferson faltering for a while but then deciding to make the purchase. Signing an agreement with the king with a French flag hanging. Meanwhile in a corner of the room the Easter bunny is resting after his busy night, it was the day after Easter that year. Thomas Jefferson leaves the signing, walks in a calendar through the block of Tuesday April 12 and Wednesday April 13 where he is greeted with a birthday cake and a tee shirt with the number 60 on it. A few years later Easter fell on April 11, the anniversary of the purchase, to remember it I wrote a parody to the song "In Your Easter Bonnet" that went "Louisiana Purchase" (In—Louis, your–si, Ea—ann, ter–a, Bonn—Pur, nnet—chase).

Another subject that intrigued me was geography. I got a puzzle of the United States. Each piece was a state and you put it on top of a star with the name of the state capital on it. When I first opened it I took each piece off one at a time to see underneath what the capital was. Then I would say it rote ten times, and then create a pictorial association with the state and the capital. I will describe four of them here, then at the end of the chapter there is a list of a few more states and their capitals, and you can try forming associations to remember.

Nebraska Lincoln. I imagined Abraham Lincoln walking through a cornfield, as there is a lot of corn in Nebraska.

Nevada, Carson City. Nevada looks like a piece of pizza, so I imagined Johnny Carson wolfing down a pizza.

Vermont, Montpelier. There is a lot of skiing in Vermont. I imagined a frustrated skier pelting the side of a mountain.

New Mexico, Santa Fe. I imagined some Santa Fe model trains I had growing up transversing New Mexico.

I was able to get pictures in my head of what each state looked like by staring at the puzzle pieces and when I put them together I would imagine they looked like something. Maine was like a dog with its ears. Florida was giving someone the thumbs down sign of disapproval. The eastern seaboard looked like a kangaroo, with its ears in Maine, its paws were Massachusetts, its pouch was the North Carolina coast, and it's leg it was hopping around on was Florida. Texas was a butterfly.

The next thing I did with the map was adding pictures of landscapes or historical events on my pictures of the states. So when I saw the state on the map I would see the picture. South Dakota was the four faces of Mount Rushmore, North Carolina was the Wright Brothers with the first plane, Washington was cherry trees etc. Doing this activity was helpful years later in Eighth Grade when we had to memorize the leading products of each state. I remembered my map and made pictures of the products on the picture of each state.

Sometimes I would create an association and add on to it periodically if more information was forthcoming. When the Apollo moon landings were occurring I would create associations for the mission. Then months later when there would be another one I would add to my own "Moon-walk" with associations for the new mission.

When Neil Armstrong and Edwin "Buzz" Aldrin landed and walked on the moon on July 20, 1969 the whole world was watching. Most people who were alive then knew the names of the astronauts because they were interested in the event. Suppose you were not born then and want to learn, how could you do it then? You could make associations. Here is how I did it.

Apollo 11. I imagined the two men standing side by side like two of the number one, therefore 11. Then one kneels down and is attacked by a strong army (kneel–Neil, strong army—Armstrong) the other changes into a cauldron (Aldrin) that is making a buzzing noise (Buzz). This is all taking place by a sea that is so tranquil there is not even a ripple on the surface. (Apollo 11 explored the region of the moon called the Sea of Tranquility). They enter the lunar module and take off, because the army scares them.

After the first landing the public interest in moon landings waned. By the last ones people would complain that their soap opera is not on today, this thing is on. However, I kept watching and following it out of personal interest.

The next mission was Apollo 12 in November 1969. I added the following associations to my story. A new spaceship appears in the sky and lands with the number 12 on it. Suddenly a storm erupts, and the formerly tranquil sea erupts and there are waves, it is now an ocean. (Apollo 12 explored the Ocean of Storms). The module lands beside the ocean and a bunch of feet with little arms descend onto the surface; the feet are comrades (Feet—Pete, comrades—Conrad). Pete Conrad was one astronaut. They are then followed out of the ship by a giant bean. However, the bean gets beaten down by the waves and is sick from the storm, so it's an ailing bean (the other astronaut was Alan Bean). The feet and bean decide the place is bad luck so they fly away. Bad luck reigned with Apollo 13. This mission for me lent itself to a chain of memory associations with 13 being bad luck. It was Apollo 13. They lifted off at 2:13 in the afternoon, and they had a cryogenic problem on the 13th of the month (April 13, 1970). I visualized the trouble in the module as emitting a red haze (Astronaut Fred Haise). Then I thought of them keeping warm in the cryogenics by exercising. After all one of them loved to go to the gym (Astronaut Jim Lovell) .The third astronaut exercised by swinging a car jack around (Jack Swigert).

With each subsequent flight I would add on to my chain of associations the names of the astronauts, the dates of the flights, and the regions explored. So I added two sets in 1971 and two more in 1972.

In the summer of 1995 I expanded the associations with Apollo 13 when I saw the movie of the same name. I now included the names of the wives, children, and the people in Mission Control. I associated the names of some actors in the show too. Now every time I think Jim Lovell I think Tom Hanks, for Commander Gene Krantz it's Ed Harris. I now added to Jack Swigert swinging a jack that the reason he was doing it was because he was angry that he had not paid his income taxes and they would be in space until after the April 15 deadline.

I looked at this as a tree of associations that grew from time to time and grew a branch outwards years later.

December 1972	Apollo 17
April 1972	Apollo 16
Jul—Aug. 1971	Apollo 15
Jan—Feb 1971	Apollo 14
April 1970	Apollo 13 __July 1995 Apollo 13 movie
November 1969	Apollo 12
July 1969	Apollo 11

This metaphor of a tree can be useful to college students as you are progressing through a course each semester. You can add a chapter's information to the tree, as you cover each subject in class. Using each chapter of a text as a layer on the tree can remind you to review each chapter each week so it will be easier when you take a test if you have reviewed periodically. It also makes it easier to relearn material, and it will be easier to recall at the time of the final if you studied each week and just added to your chain of associations.

It seemed through my grade school years I was always memorizing something. . Whether it was for school or for entertainment, I always had something my head. For my leisure I would memorize sports statistics, or T.V. trivia similar to what got me started with memorizing (the nightly lineup) Over a period of a week in Grade 5 I sneaked inside at recess and memorized the lists of birthdays that hung outside our classrooms, until I knew the birth dates of all my schoolmates in my grade.

When I was not memorizing information I would be swimming, playing baseball, and doing things that all boys do. I was a regular boy with an extraordinary memory.

What you can do

Have you ever noticed that children seem to be able to remember everything? You take your 4 year old to an aunt's house, where you have not been in a year. He immediately starts searching for a toy he played with the last time you were there. Or you go on vacation and your child remembers the name of a favorite ice cream parlor that you stopped in once last year when you were vacationing in the same spot. One reason for this is that children are not required to remember anything, so anything they remember is because they want to remember it, not because someone is forcing them. This is the same reason that anyone can remember details about their hobby. Whether it is popular culture, sports facts, types of models to build etc. if the interest is there so will the ability be.

So how does this apply to someone who has a new job, they don't like it much but it's a living, or maybe someone in college takes a job at a restaurant even though they want to work as an engineer but this job will help pay next semester's tuition. To make the menu interesting enough to bother memorizing they could first remember a time when they enjoyed a good meal similar to something on the menu and then every time they see that dish listed they recall the time they enjoyed it. Then they could create a series of pictures to connect the other items on the menu to that favorite. When they are at work with the customers they could visualize the customer riding a chicken on it's back if that is what they ordered, or if they ordered something vegetarian imagine the customer with the vegetables growing out of their hands or in their mouth. If the employee is bored with learning the procedure for opening and closing the restaurant, they could compare the procedure with how some engineering system they learned in school works. The idea again is to make the information interesting by connecting it to something that you already find interesting.

Here are some exercises as a continuation of the ones I described earlier. Try making some stories, and feel free to make them as bizarre as you want. The less likely the story could happen in real life the more effective it can be in helping you memorize. Note: There is a glossary in the back that lists every day of the year and includes celebrity birthdays. Since you may not have the same knowledge of dates that I do. I recommend using that glossary as a guide.

If you have trouble creating the pictures I would recommend that you skip to the final chapter where I outlined a seven-step process for creating the pictures.

State Capitals:

Maine—Augusta
Kansas—Topeka
South Dakota—Pierre
Florida—Tallahassee
Texas—Austin
California—Sacramento
North Dakota—Bismarck
Colorado—Denver
New York—Albany
Delaware—Dover.

Apollo Missions

Apollo 14

January 31 to February 9, 1971 moon walk on February 5 and 6.

Alan Shepherd
Edgar Mitchell
Fra Mauro region
Alan Shepherd hit a golf ball.

Apollo 15

July 26 to August 5, 1971. Moonwalks were July 31 and August 1.
First mission that the Moon Rover vehicle was used.
David Scott
James Irwin
Hadley Rille

Apollo 16

April 16 to 27, 1972. Moonwalks were April 21 through the 24th
John Young
Charlie Duke—First twin on the moon
Cayley plains

Apollo 17

December 7 to 19, 1972. First trip to include a scientist who was not a pilot.
Eugene Cernan
Jack Harrison Schmidt
Taurus Littrow region.

4

How I Memorized My Work in Junior and Senior High School

By my teenage years I had memorized so many dates, and stored so many memories of episodes in my life, that I was able to recall the last time the same combination occurred. Since the dates repeat themselves every five, six, and eleven years, starting at age 12 I was able to compare each day with what I remembered five years earlier when the same combination occurred. For example, on Friday August 4 1972 I was leaving to go on a vacation and it was a sunny day. I remember thinking "This is better than the last time August 4 fell on a Friday in 1967. It was raining and we were coming home from a vacation.

As 1972 progressed and I compared it to 1967 I realized that as I was growing up I was a much more emotional person. Twelve is an age of extreme emotions because those parts of the brain that cause our feelings develop rapidly. Twelve year olds can be happy one minute then stomp out of the room the next minute if you ask them to do the dishes. . I was no exception to this rule. One might think that intellectual people are not highly emotional, but I always was. People can be any combination of traits. A huge football player could be highly sensitive to pain and a four-foot fashion model might not be. Or a top student could also be good with people, and not a nerd who only wants to sit at the computer terminal. Stereotypes are often wrong, and life can be more interesting, and you remember more, when you do not make any assumptions but ask people how they are. When you make assumptions you are blocking your percep-tion. For example, suppose you just met someone who works making house calls repairing computers, so you stereotype him as a computer geek.

He tells you about how well he did in college, and how he follows world affairs. Then he tells you how he likes to go to the local bar on Saturday nights because they have Karaoke and he likes to get up and sing. You will probably change the subject quickly because you are assuming that he spends Saturday nights at home on his computer figuring out how to make more money. Consequentially you do not remember as much about him as you would have if you just listened to him without any assumptions.

In senior year in high school I took an accounting course. I figured since I was good with numbers I would excel at accounting and enjoy it. I found it so boring and meaningless that I was depressed for the first 50 minutes of school each day when I was in the class. I think that accounting does no have anything to do with the way I memorize. There is nothing creative about it. You just plug the numbers in. There were no creative pictures or stories to make. Although I have a lot of respect for accountants, it just was not my field.

During my teenage years I looked for meaning in terms of patterns. I compared weather in different years and tried to see patterns according to the calendar. For example, does the 6th always produce a hot summer, followed by a snowy winter? It did in 1966 and 1977.Do late Easters produce low snowfall the winter leading up to them and do early Easters produce heavy snow? This was the case in 1973—no snow fell in my area and Easter fell on April 22. In 1967 and 1978 Easter fell on March 26 and both years produced more than twice the average amount of snowfall for my area. Additionally I memorized positions of the planets and how that might impact weather; again, I picked an unusual way to make sense of things.

In secondary education you learn subjects that do not lend themselves easily to pictures. Consequentially I needed to develop the ability to make pictures out of abstract concepts. One class that gave me an opportunity to do this was eighth and twelfth grade Government class. I made stories and pictures to understand three laws in the constitution, which could easily be confused over their definition.

Habeas Corpus—Detainees seek relief from unlawful imprisonment.
Bill of Attainder—Declaring a person or group guilty of a crime without benefit of a trial.
Ex Post Facto Law—Law that retroactively changes the legal consequences of acts committed or the legal status of facts and relationships that existed prior to the enactment of the law.

I created stories to illustrate these legal concepts. For Habeas Corpus—A corpse was found covered with hay. There was one pitchfork on the ground and nine bees swarming around it (hay—bees—corpse) Habeas Corpus was addressed in Article 1 section 9 of the constitution, so I put one pitchfork and nine bees. Some might think this is a pretty gruesome way to remember something. However, anything that arouses strong feeling aids in memory. You could also use the sound effect of the bees buzzing. Someone happened to be walking by and they arrested him even though he did not commit the murder, therefore it was an unlawful imprisonment.

The prisoner sends the letter out, seeking relief from his imprisonment. Then he gets an invitation from the court to answer new proceedings. I visualize a colorful envelope with a smiley face on it like an ad. This was my visual cue for the Latin phrase Habeas Corpus ad Respondenium—An order allowing the prisoner to "Answer Proceedings". The ad requires that he testify—Habeas Corpus ad Testificandium—Then the court rules and the judgments are satisfied. Habeas Corpus ad Satisfactium Satisfacendium.

If you were learning about some of the history of the use of Habeas Corpus you could include this. April 27, 1861 President Lincoln suspended Habeas Corpus in Maryland due to riots, and local militia risings, and fear that Maryland would secede and D.C would be surrounded by enemies. I imagined Lincoln arresting rebel soldiers around the State Capital, throwing them in jail with a piece of paper with the word Habeas Corpus hovering (suspended) in the air. While in a window Ulysses S.

Grant is blowing out birthday candles with the number 3 and 9. It was his 39th birthday.

Then there is Bill Of Attainder. A bill of Attainder is a legislative act declaring a person, or persons guilty of some act without the benefit of a trial. This could easily be confused with Habeas Corpus because they both involve incarceration without a trial. Similarly, Bill of Attainder is covered in the Article 9 of the constitution, but also in Article 10. It is forbidden on the Federal Level in Article 9 and on the State level in Article 10. I will use a completely different visualization from the one used for Habeas Corpus, to avoid confusing the two.

First, there is a piece of paper with the word Bill on it. Attainder means tainted, and it's parched and wrinkled, and feels disgusting to touch. Then, a man in a tee shirt with the word Federal on it comes, and he is missing one finger. He uses the nine fingers he has to tear up the bill (One man nine fingers—Article one, Section nine). Then another paper identical to the first appears and a man with a cap that says state on it uses all ten of his fingers to tear that bill. (One-man—Ten Fingers—Article 1 section 10). The torn pieces of paper fall in two places. One is in a crowded jail and the other in an empty courtroom (The jail represents convicted—the courtroom no benefit of trial).

Originally in England, anyone who was issued a Bill Of Attainder was stripped of their property and could no longer will it to the family. The property would go to the British Crown. First I saw in my head England as it appears on the map. Then I imagined it in a jail, where an inmate is thinking about his property. I imagined a house with a lawn in the British countryside inside a cloud bubble, as they have in the comics in the newspaper. Suddenly the house disappears and there is a giant crown instead.

For Ex Post Facto Law (see definition above) I imagined a group of prisoners in their scrubs about to run a race. The problem is that when any of them nears the posts of the finish line the line moves back to another set of posts, so they are the ex posts. This also captures the idea that suddenly their sentence is more severe because they moved their crime to a more strict law.

Then there are those confusing offices in government, such as the President Pro Tempore. First, I visualized the symbol of the U.S. Presidency with the eagle. The eagle has some darts and is throwing them skillfully at a target like a pro. However, he missed one and is having a temper over it. (Presidential seal—President Pro dart thrower and temper Pro Tempore). The senate elects the President Pro Tempore—So I visualized the senate chamber and they are all pulling levers and papers flew to the seal.

Since the president pro tempore is fourth in line for the presidency, I visualized a ladder with the president on top—Nixon at the time, then Gerald Ford—The vice president—then Carl Albert the speaker of the house, then James O. Eastland The president pro tempore at the time. Now you could visualize George W. Bush at the top, Dick Chaney next, Nancy Pollizi below him, and Robert Byrd below her.

Well, enough of government and history, how about all those biological terms. I will give an example of how I memorized the parts of the eye.

The cornea, the transparent protective layer that covers the front and bends light rays through the pupil. It is the part you put your contact lenses on. Imagine corn growing on it. The corn is not facing straight up but is bent as some flowers bend to face the sun at all time, the bending is the cue that it bends light. Then there's the pupil, the dark spot you can see at the center of the eyeball. Imagine a pupil sitting at a desk there taking in "Light" information. Iris flowers surround the pupil, as the Iris is the part of the eyeball around the pupil. Behind the iris and pupil is the lens. Pictorially it looks like a prescription lens, so picturing it does not really take excessive creativity. I imagined a lens that was not hard and solid but actually changed shape, since that is what the lens does as it adjusts from near objects to far objects. Since most people are either nearsighted or farsighted I included in my story that there is a lottery for perfect lenses. Anyone who does not win must choose between getting a lens that will only work for near objects or one that only works for far objects. Behind the lens is the large part of the eye called the Vitreous Humor. In a model of a large eyeball it is about three times the size of the rest of the eye. It is the large oval shaped area. It is surrounded in the back by the retina. I thought of the retina as the retainer of the eye, since it surrounds and contains the back side like a ribbon on a package. Inside the retina are the rods and cones. They are easy to remember because they are shaped like rods and cones in the world. The rods help you see the dark. I imagined a little child inside the retina who gets his toy rods out every night. Then there are the cones, which allow us to see color. I imagined an assortment of ice cream flavors where the cones are different colors too and taste the same as their flavor. Thus I brought the sense of taste into my visualization, I imagined eating a cherry cone, lemon cone, chocolate cone.

Then you come to the Fovea. It is the part of the retina where the there is the most cones. So now I added to my visualization that the cones come from Fovea's Ice Cream Parlor. A little farther down the retina is the blind spot where there are no rods and cones because ganglia are extended like cable wires running through the wall. So I imagined that after people leave Fovea's Ice Cream Parlor they come to a dangerous intersection where there are accidents because visibility is bad. When people do make it through the intersection their nerves are usually shaken, and they wish they had opted to take a different route. So next is the optic nerve. The nerve carries information to both sides of the brain.

To remember the parts of the eye in order I created a story combining all the elements. Corn is growing on the outer layer of the eye (cornea) switching it's direction as the sun moves. Meanwhile a dark skinned teenage girl walks by on her way to school (dark skinned, black pupil) Her day starts out well because her boyfriend has left irises on each side of her desk. She is a little late because she has just been fitted for lenses, she did not win the lottery for perfect lenses in her natural eye. Plus her little brother kept her up late after dark playing loudly with his toy rods. Finally she decided to take him for Ice Cream at Fovea's as long as he will go to bed right away. She ordered a multicolored cone that was a mixture of flavors. They nearly had an accident on the way home when they passed blind spot intersection. It was worse than usual because it looked like some wires had been downed in the street there at Blind Spot. Her nerves were further fried when she remembered she had to go to the optician before school (optic nerve).

In High School much of the reading that is assigned is more complex than visualizing the sights and sounds in a story. I remember reading The Scarlet Letter by Nathaniel Hawthorne. It was easy to picture a woman walking down the street with a scarlet letter in front, and I was able to understand the feeling of shame she must have felt. Some people with good memory skills might have trouble with understanding morals and abstract concepts, but I seemed to understand them by incorporating feelings into the pictures

So I have given examples of how I used my memory skills and imagination to handle different subjects at school. Perhaps surprisingly I did not always use them for school. There were some subjects that I found so boring, such as the aforementioned accounting course, that I did not bother to use the skills. I was a fairly good student but probably could have been better.

Children and adolescents seem to have different interests and values at different periods of their growing up. They may spend some years emphasizing sports or social life, other years emphasizing school, then there are the ones who do nothing but get in trouble. During my Junior High years I was strongly into my studies and used my techniques to be a top student. In High School I was into my studies at times, but at other times I was developing socially and more involved with activities.

5

The College Years

After much debate over what to do with my life, I settled on being a psychology major at La Salle University. I figured I could combine counseling, where I use my empathy skills, with research where I would use my numerical skills. I enjoyed learning about how the mind works and enjoyed my religion and literature courses as well. I was discovering the joys of abstract thinking, interpreting stories, psychological theories, and religious precepts.

In some ways, my thoughts on different psychological theorists were ahead of my time. This was the late 1970's and I remember thinking that Freud's ideas of the unconscious were unhelpful. The idea that 98% of out thoughts and feelings are caused by our interpretation of events that happened before we were old enough to remember them did not appeal to me. Freud seemed to think that the most we could do is learn to live with the way our early childhood traumas affected us. I thought that in the future people would be unwilling to spend every day for seven years or more in a therapist's office and all they would get is learning to deal with troubled primordial unconscious impulses. I liked cognitive therapy where you change your thoughts and beliefs and then your feelings and behaviors change too. I also liked Rational Emotive Therapy with Albert Ellis. I remember in my sophomore year taking Abnormal Psychology. The professor gave us a list of Albert's original irrational ideas. Which he believed is the cause of all human misery. I saw rational emotive therapy and cognitive therapy as quick gateways to happiness and success.

For reasons that would seem obvious, I considered History as a major, and would have stayed with History if there were more you could do with it. During the later part of my high school years and the entirety of my college years I worked in a museum in Center City Philadelphia called the Balch Institute. It was a museum for ethnic studies, and my mother was the Education Coordinator. One day I was brought into the director's office and saw a familiar looking portrait of George Washington. The director explained that that is the original Gilbert Stuart painting, probably the most well known portrait of George Washington. You see a picture of it in your high school history books. I stood there looking at it feeling like royalty, and wondering how it landed on the floor of a museum director's office during the bicentennial year Wednesday December 29, 1976. Then four years later on Thursday November 20, 1980 I went to the Pennsylvania Historical Society on a class assignment to learn about a historic document. All that was required was that we talk to someone at the Historical Society about a chosen document. I walked in my best suit and tie and in my most professional voice asked the curator to tell me about Daniel Shay's letter to the farmers authorizing the rebellion in the winter of 1787. This rebellion ultimately led to the Constitutional Convention that summer. Our teacher told us that we could not expect to actually be shown the documents, but we could inquire about them and write a report about it. Well, I must have made a very professional impression on the curator, because he led me to a bench in the reference area and presented the document for me to observe. I sat there and imagined I was stewing over the Articles of Confederation and finding the right choice of words to incite all farmers in the new land to rebel against the feckless government. That was an event I probably would have remembered even with an average memory.

Essentially I used the same techniques as before to do my History paper on Shay's Rebellion as I had used in High School to pass tests. Shays led a rebellion of farmers from Western Massachusetts because they were being taxed excessively to pay the state's wartime debt. I imagined a map of Massachusetts with some farmer faces on the western side groaning over a large mound of money on their heads. I felt the heaviness of the money, which represented the burden of taxes. Then I imagined some farm buildings on the Western side being pounded by a gavel, this represented the courts taking away their farms when they did not pay. The state government was taxing the farmers to pay eastern Massachusetts creditors who lent them now depreciated bonds to finance the war. I added to the story money floating from the western to the eastern part of the state and when it stopped coming the gavel pounded the farm.

Then I imagined an army burning down the courthouse. as they marched on the courts. What happened next was the Nationalists including Henry Knox informed George Washington that we are moving towards anarchy. This required no techniques, just that I imagined George Washington looking terrified as he gazed out his Mount Vernon window and agreed to preside at the Constitutional Convention the following summer in Philadelphia.

I did another paper in that class on the Monroe Doctrine. It was signed on Tuesday December 2, 1823. It proclaimed that European powers could no longer colonize or interfere with the affairs of the Americas.

First I visualized a doctor counting his rows of money. (Money row—Monroe Doctor—Doctrine). Then a giant map of Europe comes alongside the doctor and a giant map of the United States on the other. The Europe map lunges towards the U.S. map but the built row of money prevents Europe from getting to the United States. This picture could be interpreted a number of different ways. Europe is trying to colonize the U.S by lunging, but the money row and doctor serve as a wall to prevent it.

We can add to this a picture of the situation, which led to the passage of the Doctrine. Spain was trying to regain her new world colonies. Russia and France wanted to help but England refused to get involved.

On the picture of Europe, I visualized Spain breaking off and trying to move against the wall to the U.S. France and Russia break off too and push Spain towards the U.S. Of course the doctor's money row keep Spain back. England stands there and watches and the upper portion of England shakes like someone shaking his or her head. Spain then grows an arm and hand, and snaps it's fingers as someone will do when they are frustrated. The U.S. then grows a face and breathes a sigh of relief. (Thus bringing emotion to the picture).

I discovered that I could use my techniques even in my psychology courses. In one of my more advanced courses we had to learn the names of some of the more obscure contributors in the field (note: Now this is required learning in Psychology 101) here is the list and how I memorized it.

Christine Ladd Franklin—PHD at Johns Hopkins mid 1880's. Degree in 1926 because they did not give degrees to women before that, Contribution: Evolutionary theory of color vision.

Mary Whiton Calkins—Doctorate at Harvard under William James, contribution: Psychology laboratory at Wellesley College. Developed Paired—Associates test in memory. First female president of American Psychological Association in 1905.

Margaret Floy Washburn Ph.D from Cornell Contributions: Taught at Vassar College. Wrote The Animal Mind, and Movement and Mental Imagery.

Francis Cecil Sumner—First African American to earn a Ph.D in psychology from Clark University Contributions: Translated over 3000 articles from German, French, and Spanish. He chaired the psychology department at Howard University. He is known as the "father" of African American Psychology.

Jorge Sanchez Contribution: Studies on the biases in intelligence testing. Cultural and language differences hinder the performance of Hispanic students on IQ tests.

This exercise can be helpful not only in doing schoolwork but in remembering facts about people you meet. Therefore it can be good on the job or in your personal relationships. Nothing flatters someone more than if you remember their name, and it adds to the flattery if you remember facts about them even when you have not encountered them for a while.

Here is how I memorized the names and facts about these contributors.

Christine Ladd Franklin (A young lad is playing by a pristine lake, there is a statue of Benjamin Franklin in the middle) Then the City of Baltimore grows around the lake and the lad changes into a woman hopping from toilet to toilet (Baltimore and hopping toilets for Johns Hopkins). Then she stands in a line with a group of men; there is a banner above her head that says 1880's. The men are all being handed a metal replication of the Hippocratic symbol but they ignore her. Then the sign changes to 1926 and they give her one. (Refused doctorate in 1880's but granted in 1926) Then she is writing on a piece of paper, a thought cloud appears and it had a picture of a monkey and a rainbow with dull colors above his head. Then to the right is a person with a bright with a bright rainbow above their head. (Her theory is of the evolution of color vision).

Mary Whiton Calkins (Someone is whittling and calking at the fireplace that has Christmas decorations on it. Merry—(Mary) Christmas decorations—Whittling and calking Whiton Calkins). Again you see a line of people but this time with a Harvard sign on top—and only the men are given the Hippocratic symbol. Then she goes away to a well, and easily draws up a building replica that says Psychology laboratory. (Well easily Wellesley College—Psychology laboratory) Then she needs to draw the building replica very high because attached underneath are several pairs of things (paired associate test).
Then she is approached by a group of people in academic gowns and you hear the music "Hail to the chief" and a banner that says American Psychological Association"

Margaret Floy Washburn (A woman gritting her teeth as she uses a toy cleaning set to wash something that is Burned). Then you see some corn in the shape of the letter L and she is given the Hippocratic symbol. She says I can make money faster, (Vasser), if I teach. She then finds herself taking notes as people dissect animal brains, The Animal Mind, and also teaches a dance class where you imagine things as you dance Movement and Mental Imagery.

Francis Cecil Sumner. First I pictured Cecil the Seasick Sea Serpent dancing in the summer son (Francis—dancing then Cecil and summer). Then Cecil turns into a black man in front of a University building and Clark Kent gives him his Hippocratic symbol, the rest of the recipients are white. (He was the first African American to get the Doctorate from Clark). He then flies out to a map of Europe, and lands respectively on Germany, France, and Spain. Then papers fly from him on the map back to the U.S. (He translated from those three languages). Then he flies back and sits in a chair with a banner that says Psychology Department on top. (He chaired the department at Howard University). I then pictured the stork flying in and bringing him a baby named African American Psychology.

Jorge Sanchez, I pictured a chest being filled with sand (sand chest—Sanchez) the chest grows arms and his hoarding hay around it (hoarding hay—Jorge). Then a piece of paper appears that says I.Q. test. The chest turn into a man and then a group of Hispanic people who march around with strike like signs chanting unfair culture, unfair language.

This now completes the examples of how I used the memory techniques to master my schoolwork. Additionally I used these techniques in graduate school to remember the by laws of the American Psychological Association. I continued to use my skills to memorize anything which I had an interest in. I memorized the release dates of all the Beatles albums and songs, the names of Marx brothers movies, and who else starred in them. All of the American space flights not previously mentioned from Alan Shepherd in Freedom 7 all the way to the first few shuttle flights in the 1980's.

What You Can Do

Making connections with things is an obvious way to enhance your memory. When I was glancing at the Shays document I used my imagination to enhance and deepen the memory of the experience. Some people might have just looked at the document, noted anything they could decipher with the quill pen writing, wrote it down and gone home. I imagined being Daniel Shays, imagined a desk in a farmhouse by a fire, imagined myself being angry with the government, and imagined a group of farmers starting an insurrection. So the entire experience was much more emotional that it could have been if I had not done that. The more emotion you bring into memorizing something the better it will stick with you. It can be just as important as using sights and sounds as memory cues. You may recall that there was one exercise where I incorporated taste into the visualization (The ice cream colors) The more senses you employ the more likely you will remember everything in the visualization.

Her is an example of another person who was a little known pioneer in psychology. See if you can create a story to remember him.

Albert Sydney Beckham—He did studies on intelligence and showed how it correlates positively with success in various occupational fields. He established the first psychology laboratory in Howard University.

6

Fascination with Weather

By the time I entered my teen years, I had memorized the weather every day for several years. When I first started this I would visualize the letters and numbers of the month, day, and year on the ground the size of skyscrapers. Then I would imagine them affected by the weather. For example, Sunday July 3, 1966 and Monday July 4 were both red in the calendar because they were a Sunday and a holiday. I imagined they became red because it was red hot on those days. Then on Wednesday September 14 it poured rain. I imagined the 1 and the 4 dripping wet and probably glad to fly off the face of the earth at midnight. Snowy days always had snow covering the tops of the numbers and snow on the ground in the picture. I do not know what I would have done if I lived in a climate where the weather changes frequently throughout a typical day. When I was on a 1994 vacation in Ireland in one day, Monday April 18 the weather changed from snow flurries, rain, and sun all in the space of a few hours. Then I have heard the in New England if you don't like the weather, wait a minute. I guess I would have had to find a way to break it down into hours instead of days in those circumstances.

As a child of the sixties, I grew up in a time when temperatures tended towards the cold side. Winters tended to always be cold and snowy (more that in recent years), and summers tended to be warm and pleasant but, except for 1966, without major heat waves. Spring came late and autumn came early. This was a regular pattern during the first ten years of my life, and I never knew anything different.

In the early seventies the weather changed to a warmer pattern. I remember beginning a new school in fifth grade and during the first month of school it was so hot that the teacher frequently let us out for extra recess (note: We had not moved south) Then at the end of that month it was on the news that this September 1970 set a record for the most 90 plus degree days in a September. A year later in 1971 we set a record for the warmest October. This seemed like a freak of nature. . Then when summer 1973 arrived it was the hottest summer since 1900. I remember thinking that I like this better than the colder weather. However, I wondered how the balance of nature would be affected if global temperatures became higher, and I wondered how the land masses would sink into the Ocean if the polar ice caps melted. I was predicting the greenhouse effect before it became fashionable.

After the no snow winter of 1973 there was the no gas winter of 1974. OPEC led us to believe there was an oil shortage. This also led to beginning Daylight Savings time on January 6. The president and congress decided that we use more oil in the evening so we would use less if it stayed light longer in the afternoon. The problem was that most people now were up getting ready for work and school in the dark. Even though that was a mild winter it seemed cold because of going to school earlier. In 1975 we had even milder winter temperatures and little snow. I remember thinking that those years must have been a nightmare for the ski resorts they must have had to get new snow making machines every year and having days where people had to ski in mud. Then people did not go to the slopes because the gas would cost too much to get there.

Although I began noting the daily weather since I was six years old, I now was interested in records. I found an almanac at the library and memorized heat waves, snowstorms, snowfall totals each winter. I memorized the hottest and coldest months, years etc. During the rest of the 70's I was intrigued by all the interesting weather that happened. In the summer of 1974 the Midwest was so dry that they experienced dust storms for the first time since the 1930's. So while Nixon was resigning the Midwest farmers were wondering how to salvage their crops. Is it any wonder that many people were depressed in the 70's?

On Easter weekend 1976 the Philadelphia area experienced 90 + temperatures from Good Friday April 16 to Easter Monday April 19. Then the highs were in the 80's for the next three days. Conversely the summer of 1976 was mild. So it was pleasant for all the tourists who came to Philadelphia. Of course, the cool summer temperatures and Bicentennial was a nightmare for the New Jersey Shore Merchants. However, they were compensated the following summer with the Bicentennial being over and a nine-day heat waver from July 13—21.

After the mild summer of '76 the fall and winter temperatures plummeted to record lows. For four months (October 10, 1976 to February 9, 1977) the temperatures along the east coast were consistently below average. November of 1976 was the coldest November on record, January 1977 was the coldest January and coldest calendar month on record. The previous coldest month was February of 1934. The coldest autumn on record, previously it was 1903. It was also the coldest winter on record, inching out 1962-63.

The cold marathon was followed by several months of generally above average temperatures. A very warm spring followed in 1977, then a hot summer with a heat wave from July 13-21 where the temperature rose to 90 or above each day. It was interesting that 1977 saw the first subzero temperatures in Philadelphia since 1963,—4 on January 17 and—3 on January 18. Then July 21 was the first 100-degree day since July 4, 1966. As a psychologist I look at 1977 as a bipolar year. Bipolar is a mental disorder, which includes extremes of mood. They can be very depressed at times and man icky at other times.

My interest in weather declined in the 1980's, as I was concentrating on college and starting a career. Also there seemed to be fewer incidents of record braking weather. We did have a significant day on Cold Sunday, January 17, 1982 when the high was 0 and the low was—7. Then on January 22, 1984 the low was—6.

In the middle and late 1980's the weather in general began to get warmer again, as it had been in the early and mid 1970's. I began to develop an interest again in the summer of 1988. Suddenly we had a record hot summer and we broke several specific records for heat. We had five days of the temperature reaching 100 or above. June 22, July 10 and 11—100. July 16 and 17—102. We also had the longest heat wave up to that time. 19 days from July 28 to August 15. That summer there were no elderly people saying "It don't get hot like it used to". That summer was when the term "Greenhouse Effect' became vogue.

As a hot weather person I really enjoyed the hot 90's. Interestingly the temperature became obediently warmer just as the 90's were beginning. December of 1989 was record cold nationwide and the shift in the jet stream brought warmer temperatures right on New Years Day 1990. January was 15 degrees warmer than December had been and the temperatures hit the 80's for five days in mid March. By the end of 1990 America had its warmest calendar year on record. However, this has been bested in 1998, and 2002 through 2006 were all warmer than 1990 nationwide.

In my area 1991 was even warmer. In May we had a nine-day heat wave and it was the hottest May on record. I remember wondering if there is a balance in world temperatures. The Gulf war ended in March 1991 and Saddam Hussein's men blew up Kuwaiti oil refineries. The effects of that were felt there for several months afterwards as the fire and oil created a block in the stratosphere so the heat from the sun could not get in. Consequentially they had their coldest May on record. Did we get the compensation here in the eastern United States with a hot May?

By the time I was in my 30's in the 1990's I was busy with my career in human services, enjoying the single life on the weekends, and had little free time to sit and memorize anything. However, memorizing the weather and events had become second nature so I did it habitually without much seeming effort. When you get into the habit of doing anything it becomes what we call "second nature" the more ingrained the less you have to think about doing it and just do it. Can you imagine how difficult life would be if we had to think "breathe in, breathe out" or "Put one foot in front of the other, now put the other foot in front". Or imagine if we had to look at a map every time we went to work or to get home from work. We do not have to do these things because it becomes habitual. For me memorizing information got to where I never had to sit down and put effort into it. I just did it from habit.

The 1988 record for the hottest summer was broken three times in the 1990's. 1991, 1994, and 1995 were progressively hotter. 1993 and 1999 were in the top 10. Now, heading into the new millennium the summer of 2002 was just as hot as 1988 and 2005 was hotter.

My attitude towards cold weather and snow is that it is okay but I can do without it. The greenhouse effect has been evident in recent years in some mild winters. In the northeast, the winters of 1991, 1998, and 2002 were all in the top 10. Nationwide the winter of 1992 saw the mildest temperatures and the lowest snowfall. This record was broken in the winter of 2000.

As I memorized this information I linked it to other events in the news and in my life. I would include the weather in my links with each date. Here is another example like the one in the previous chapter.

Monday January 17, 1977—The day of Gary Gilmore's execution in a Utah state prison. We had late arrival in my high school due to teacher meetings. In swim class we took a canoe into the water and I hid under it with three friends. I had been on a skiing trip the previous Saturday the 15th at Hahn Mountain in the Pocono's. Getting ready for school I heard the song "Blue Jeans" on the radio. Other hits at that time were "Torn Between two lovers" by Mary McGregor. "Weekend in New England" by Barry Manilow, and "Blinded by the Light" by Manfred Mann's Earth Band. It is interesting to note that the 70"s were called the "Yawning 70's" yet most people from my generation love that music.

As you can see I linked up several types of topics together which have no obvious connection. For example, as I listened to "Blue Jeans" I put the date in a parity of the lyric. As I heard "Put on your jeans, and come on ride with me" I played in my head "Today is January seventeenth". Then when I arrived at school I repeated the date in my head as I was walking behind a couple in the hallway and they were talking about Gary Gilmore. Then when I was in the pool messing around with the canoe I thought of the irony of being in a pool on a subzero day and wondered what it would be like to be outdoors on January 17. Consequentially, on my story for that date I combined my own experience with the news and weather.

First Gary Gilmore is wearing blue jeans before going before the firing squad. The squad is late getting there because they had a meeting. One member of the firing squad wants to get finished so he can go canoeing even in the cold. Another, whose name is Hahn is in a hurry to go skiing. Meanwhile a man comes on a double motorcycle and gives one to Gary and they escape. The problem is that they both are heading to Mr. Macgregor's farm to take his daughter Mary out. It takes them until the weekend to get there to New England where the sunlight on the snow is blinding.

Besides being an expert on memory. I have always been a reflective person. I would wonder about how various events affect each other. This included how weather affects people. For example, many people get sad or depressed on a cloudy or rainy day. I wondered if they were more depressed on the first rainy day after a sunny day than if it was the third or fourth cloudy or rainy day in a row. The corollary would be if people would be happier on the first sunny day after a rainy day than they would be on the fifth sunny day in a row.

Additionally, I was interested in how weather patterns affected the balance of nature. Every year I would note which date the crocuses, daffodils, etc. would begin and finish blooming. I noted the date the sycamore, birches and maple leaves would sprout. This was more variable than animal migrations, which as legend has it would always migrate on the same day of the year, The Buzzards on March 15 to Hickory Ohio, and the swallows on March 19 to Capistrano California. In my area, I have observed maple leaves sprouting as early as February 25 in 2002, and as late as April 15 in 1978. While it would seem obvious that flowers would bloom and leaves would sprout earlier after a mild winter, I observed an additional pattern. When snow and cold weather occur in January and early February, then it gets much warmer in late February and early March, everything blooms and sprouts quickly. This happened in 1976, 77, 79. 83, 85, 94, 2000, and 2004. My hunch is that the snow protects the ground when it is cold then the snow melts in late February producing necessary irrigation.

I did make some informal observations about human behavior and the weather. When the temperature goes up after being cold for a while people get irritable. I observed that in school on February 10, 1977. After months of cold it got warm and the kids suddenly got mean. Years later, when I worked in a psychiatric hospital it seemed that more patients were admitted during mild weather than during very cold weather. In December 1989 we had six patients at one time. In January when it got much warmer we were filled to capacity of 26 within two days. Similarly hot summer weather seemed to cause people with mental illness to be more exacerbated than during mild summer weather.

I noticed that people's personalities seemed to be affected by the weather on the day they were born and the first few days or weeks afterwards. Whenever a new patient was admitted to any facility I worked in I would look at their chart and memorize their birth date (And add them to my stream of associations about that date.) I noticed that people who were born around the same time would often be admitted and discharged from treatment around the same time. Could it be that there is something to astrology, just a thought. For example, we might have three or four people admitted within a week who were born July 7, 1961, July 16, 1961 July 20, 1961 and July 28, 1961. They would all enter treatment within a week of each other and leave within a week of each other.

So what does this have to do with the effects of the weather? I noticed over a long period of time that there was a higher incidence of people born during very cold winters that would be admitted to treatment. When I worked for a geriatric facility there was a high number of patients born in January of 1918, which was an extremely cold January. When I was working on adolescent and adult facilities there was a high number of patients born in the winters of 1977, 1978, 1982 and 1984 and most of them were born during the coldest periods of these winters. I wondered if, although as infants they were probably kept in heated areas the cold still circulated inside and there were probably periods when they had to be taken outside. They may have been traumatized from that. I do not want to scare anyone who was born on a cold day. Maybe the cold, which was such a contrast to the womb would traumatize someone and make him or her vulnerable to traumas when they were older. However, if you had a nice life otherwise it probably does not matter. If you did have traumatic experiences in your life you can benefit from counseling.

What You Can Do

This chapter was an illustration of relating unrelated factors. First there were weather facts, and then I related them to music, an execution, water sports, and psychiatry. All of these unrelated subjects suddenly became related as I pulled them together for the singular purpose of memorizing weather facts. You could do the following.

1. Take a subject that you are interested in, and one that you have a moderate amount of knowledge about. You do not have to be an expert, just know some facts, whether it's sports trivia, origami, the oboe etc.

2. Take a subject you are not interested in but think you should know more about it. Maybe it is your weak subject in school, an interest your significant other wishes you could share.

3. Find imaginative ways to learn the new subject by making up stories, which connect it to the old info, similar to the exercise in the previous chapter.

In this chapter I expressed that, despite having a good memory I did struggle with the decision of what to study. If you are struggling with a decision you have to make, here is a technique that could help. Get into a relaxed position where you will not be distracted. Visualize each possibility of what you are trying to decide. For example, if you are in college trying to pick a major spend a few minutes imagining yourself working in each field. The one that you feel the best visualizing is likely the major you should choose.

7

How the Memory Skills Affected Me Socially

Some of you who are reading this might be thinking "What a Sorry man, Is this all he does is sit around and memorize things? "Is he autistic"? Although I have similar abilities to an autistic savant, which is someone who has extraordinary mental abilities in one or more areas but is extremely deficient in other areas I do not have any of the other traits of autistic people. People with autism do not desire human contact, and they have trouble reading other people's social cues. Many of them hate to be touched.

In the movie "The Rain Man" Dustin Hoffman plays an autistic savant who can do what I do with the dates and has a plethora of additional skills, such as counting the toothpicks on the floor. Then he is almost completely lacking is social skills. Although that movie was an excellent depiction of the skills, bizarre mannerisms, and obsessions of an autistic savant, such as his need to watch "The People's Court", it is unrealistic to assume that in one week a man who has been autistic for more than 50 years could develop some affections for his brother. Towards the end of the movie he refers to his brother as his main man and shows some affection towards him. This could not happen in reality. I think autistic people can be helped to come out if their autism in intervened early enough, within the first couple of years of life, but not if intervention does not begin until adulthood.

Some people think that with a good memory other areas of life might be compromised, the studies conducted on this subject are meager. There were some skilled mneumonists in the past, Inodi, Diamindi, and Ishahara in which their minds and skills were studied, but no studies were done on whether they lacked or possessed social skills to the degree that others do. Then there was the Russian mneumonist Aleksandr Romanovich Luria who had a condition called synesthia. This is a condition where the senses get mixed together and it creates colors when a sound is heard . With Luria his synesthia allowed him to have a phenomenal memory where he remembered the details of everything by associating them with the enmeshment of sights and sounds in the unique way he experienced them. He might hear a word and see a splash of red or orange.

For him, it was difficult to keep his mind in reality because the images would be so strong that he would be unable to focus on a conversation happening in front of him. This is what happens to people who are thinking so hard in their head that they may not develop social skills because their focus is elsewhere. If the person with the memory skills is not autistic, it is likely that they can be sociable but have just concentrated on other things.

I did display some of these tendencies as a child. I had some bizarre mannerisms and did not like to be touched. I did not make the effort to befriend others until my adolescence and young adulthood. I had a few friends as a child, but they were children who reached out to me. I continued to be shy in high school, and then in college I really worked on being more sociable. I liked people, whereas autistic people are indifferent to others. However, with all my special abilities I was tired of the first thing anyone noticed about me was "You're shy", "You're passive" "You're introverted". Now I am in the counseling profession, which requires a high degree of social skills.

My slow social development was likely due to being so preoccupied with what was inside my head that I did not focus on the things necessary to develop social skills. The difference between Luria and I was that once I realized that I lacked social skills, I wanted to develop them. I learned to focus outward and pay attention to people and how I presented to them, simply by choice.

Even as a child I was sociable and friendly with select people, namely my family and any child who treated me well. I was always good at reading people's facial expressions and moods when I chose to, although most of the time I was in my own head. When I talked to someone I would note if they appeared bored, then I would change the subject. If they appeared angry I would either give them space or change to a lighter topic. Autistic people have no ability to read others facial expressions as clues to their mood. There is a branch of Autism called Asperser's Syndrome. These children are proficient at one subject and they go and talk to everyone about it indiscriminately, whether the person seems interested or not. I am only comfortable talking to someone about topics of mutual interest.

Autistic people have no feelings towards other people, except fear that the other might touch them or come too close. However, they have no perception about how the other person must feel. I, conversely, have always been very compassionate, if someone was sad I would want to cheer him or her up. If someone were happy I would feel joy with him or her.

How did my memory skills affect my sociability and view of people? I included in my date knowledge the behavior of people and on what date they performed the behavior. This can really make or break a relationship. Here are some hypothetical examples. If you say to someone "Remember Thursday February 6, 2003 when you could not wait to tell me that our department was the scapegoat at work? Of course, that was during your nasty period which lasted from November 6, 2002, the day you told me I was being written up to September 22, 2003 when you said you were sick of me because I was twelve minutes late coming to supervision, and If I remember correctly, you accused one of my coworkers of being an idiot on Thursday March 6, accused me of taking long breaks on Friday April 4, Told me that I should not have kept this client on Wednesday May 7, told me I did not deserve employee of the month award on Thursday June 5, yelled that I could not leave early on Thursday July 3, accused me of taking a long break on Tuesday August 5, and accused me of some office vandalism on Friday September 5. So it all must have been your time of the month". When you include the date it has a much stronger impact, and the more detail the more insulting. "Remember the time you called me a nudge when all I did was ask you boy if he wanted to be the mummy who gets buried when we were at the beach. It was Wednesday August 9, 2006.

I guess the beach is not the place for someone with Obsessive Compulsive Disorder, It's too much fun for you". Remembering the date when they ruined a fun time can really annoy or hurt someone. Frequently, when I was growing up, I would remind people I knew of times they were rude and obnoxious. "That was a year ago today when you said I have been no good for two weeks." Boy did I get some interesting reactions to this. People would look at me like they had egg yolk on their face. In all fairness, I also remembered when good events occurred and reminded people on the anniversary date. I now realize that people must have really been hurt by my remembering the bad times and things they did. Nothing is more insulting than remembering vivid details about something someone did wrong. The corollary is that nothing is more flattering than remembering someone's birthday or something positive about them in vivid detail. "So it is now Twenty years ago today that I started my first job post college. I never could have gotten this far if you had not provided so much encouragement, Remember Sunday March 25, 1973 when you sat me down and talked about all the advantages to doing well at school" That kind of remembering makes people feel good.

What You Can Do

In the early and middle years of school most children get specific ideas about what they are good at and not good at. One might be good at sports but not good at school. Another might be good at music but not good at sports. In middle school they learn very specifically where they stand socially. Consequentially by the time someone reaches the age of 18 they have a strongly defined self image which includes where they stand in intelligence, either they will go to college, learn a trade, get married and raise children etc. Everyone has an idea as to whether they are an introvert or extrovert.

The problem with this is that most people don't change their ideas when they get older. If someone would like to be more sociable as an adult than they were as a teenager they can decide to change if they want. Or if someone did not go to college when they were younger they can go at 30, 40 or 50. Sometimes there are people who have a professional career and in mid life decide to quit being a doctor and open a restaurant. The first thing you need to do is to decide it is possible to make the desired change and then go and do it. Then use some memory techniques as I have described here to learn how to do the desired undertaking.

8

Where Was I?

Everyone remembers where he or she was the day of Princess Diana's death on Sunday August 31, 1997. Then five days later where they were when they heard of Mother Theresa's death. Then there was Tuesday 9/11, the Columbia Disaster on Saturday February 1, 2003. And Catholics remember Saturday April 2, 2005 when Pope John Paul died. Older people (I don't want to offend anyone) remember the Challenger explosion on Tuesday January 28, 1986. Before that there was Friday November 22, 1963 when Kennedy was assassinated. I must confess that even though I was three and a half I do not remember Kennedy, but many people remember where they were, whom they were with, and what they were doing. That is because these events have a high emotional charge for you. You probably also remember where you were when you heard of a relative's birth and death.

By attaching emotional significance to many events I am able to remember where I was during most news events that I ever heard about. I was working down the shore in the Arcade on the Bicentennial Day At 2:00 P.M., which was the official time the declaration was adopted, I glanced out onto the beach and saw everyone holding hands. Ten days later on Wednesday July 14 I was again working there at night, when I heard someone say that the peanut farmer Jimmy Carter got the Democratic Nomination. Then, on Monday July 19 around 4:00 I heard on the arcade radio speaker that a Romanian Gymnast, Nadia Comanici just scored a perfect 10 on the uneven parallel bars at the Montreal Olympics. Four years almost to the day later, Monday July 21, 1980 I was on the train coming home from a summer job in Philadelphia when I read in the paper that Nadia fell off the bars in the Moscow Olympic Games.

My memory includes where I was when I heard of more obscure news events. I was visiting a psychiatric client at his daytime therapy program on Wednesday July 24, 2002 when I heard about the miners who were trapped in Pennsylvania. I was at a party at the shore on Tuesday July 1, 1997 when I heard that actor Robert Mitchum died. Three years later I was on the beach Saturday July 1, 2000 when I heard that Walter Mathau died. I could go on and on.

9

Is There Anything to Astrology?

Although for all of my life I assumed that astrology was nothing to place any credence in. I was curious enough to memorize the signs, compatibilities etc. in both our Western occidental system and the Asian animal system. Since I knew so many people's birthdays it was easy for me to evaluate people I knew and see if they matched their signs.

For my own part, my birthday is May 21 so I am on the cusp of two very different signs, Taurus and Gemini. I have a strong drive to accomplish things, and I always stay with a project until I have completed it. Those are Tauran traits. Gemini's are highly intelligent and articulate. So I have that as a Gemini trait. When I am at a party or a social event I tend to circulate and gab with everyone, very different from when I was a child and teenager.

Since our system is based on the time of year you were born, I wonder if other factors pertaining to when you were born could influence how someone is. Maybe Aquarians are smart because during the second trimester, when the brain forms (For them it would be August through October) the mother gets the best nutrients as the most newly harvested fruits and vegetables are marketed and consumed. Maybe babies born in March have the highest incidence of mental illness (but not everyone born in March, this was based on observations of birth dates of clients I worked with) because their brains are first formed during the first cold wave of the season. The mother suddenly breathing in suddenly colder air could affect the fetus's neural development. There could be many other factors some of which I alluded to in a previous chapter.

There could be a way to test if the astrological factors are due to natural influences on the time of year. See if people who were born in the southern hemisphere have the attributes of the opposite sign from when they were born. For example, would a Leo born in Sydney Australia be like an Aquarian born in New York City. Since there seasons are the opposite of ours.

When I learned the Asian system, I concluded that seasonal factors could not account for the differences, because each animal rules for an entire year. According to their system, I am a rat (1960). Rats are leaders; they have good memories, and are good writers. They tend to be nervous but hide it well. I have all these traits. However, rats tend to be cliquish. I am more a person who pays attention to everyone, and I do not like to exclude or ignore anyone.

With my memory for people's birthdays, I was able to take each person I knew personally, and see if they fit their astrological profiles. After analyzing more than 200 people, people I knew personally, as well as movie stars, politicians, professional athletes, etc, I concluded that astrology is just a game of chance. Many people have the traits they are supposed to, but many do not.

For example: People born in the year of the Ram cannot manage their money. I know several rams. 1907 my grandfather 1931 an uncle, and 1979 a friend, they all manage or managed their money very well. My 1931 uncle raised 6 children, has 3 houses and put two through college on one income. My grandfather kept his job and raised three children through the great depression. My friend is a conscientious coupon clipper. She made enough money giving children harp lessons to buy a condo in an expensive area at the Jersey Shore when rates were highest. Then again I know Aquarians who are sociable and not intellectual. I could go on and on.

So with all this ability to remember dates and events, I kept track of whether other people were having good or bad years, and whether their fortune or misfortune matched the kind of year they were supposed to be having, according to the Asian animal zodiac. Here are the basic rules. It goes in twelve-year cycles or dozen cades, because there are twelve signs. You are most compatible with the signs that are four ahead of you or four behind you. You are least compatible with the sign opposite you. The kind of year you have is similar. You have a good year when it is the year of your sign, or the year of a compatible sign. You have a bad year when it is the year of your opposite sign. You are to different degrees compatible with other signs and other years. There are also five elements which rule for two-year period, the element that ruled during your year controls or is controlled by another element. If it's a year the element you control rules than you will have a good year. However, if it is a year the element that controls you rules you can have a rough year.

Generally, you have a good year every four years, because they are years that either your sign or a friendly sign of yours rules. Generally speaking if you were born in a leap year you have your best years in leap years. For everyone, each year you have a birthday that is a multiple of four you have a good year. Every year you are halfway to a multiple of 12 you have a bad year, for example, the years you turn 6, 18, 30, 42, 54, and 66 are bad years. Unfortunately you only have a stellar year when the animal sign and element are extremely favorable every 20 years. Fortunately you only have an extremely unfavorable year when you turn 6 and 66.

Some good years are the years you turn 16, favorable sign, unfavorable element so not as good, 20, 24 stellar year, favorable sign, favorable element 28,32 favorable sign, neutral element. 36 favorable sign, unfavorable element, 40 favorable sign, neutral element, 44 favorable sign, favorable element, 48,52 favorable sign, neutral element,56 favorable sign, unfavorable element 60 favorable sign, neutral element,64 favorable sign and element,

The year you turn 6 would be a horrible year because you have an unfavorable sign and unfavorable element, 18,30,42 would be unfavorable sign, and neutral element, 54 unfavorable sign but favorable element, 66 horrible, same as 6. So, based on this system you start first grade and graduate from high school during two of your worst years. For example, the 2001 Metal Snakes will be starting school during the year of the fire boar 2007. Boar is opposite of Snake and fire controls metal. So it's a really bad year. Then the 1989 Earth Snakes are graduating from high school and starting work or college or college this year with an unfavorable sign and neutral element. Note: The sign generally has more impact than the element.

Meanwhile the 1943 Water Rams or goats, the 1963 Water Cats or bunnies, and the 1983 Water Boars will have their stellar years this year. They are all signs compatible with Boar and Water controls fire. The 1951 Metal Cats and 1971 Metal Boars will not have quite as good a year since Fire controls Metal. Likewise the 1953 Water Snakes will not have as bad a year as other Snakes because their element is favorable, Watch out 1941 Metal Snakes.

So how should we restructure society? Should we move the grades back a year so that starting school and graduating are not during bad years? Maybe we should keep the retirement age at 65 so they can get their stellar year at 64 out of them but get them out of the workforce before the horrific year when they turn 66 and foul everything up.

As a rat I have had good things happen to me during horse years, and bunny years, which is not supposed to happen. I have had occasional challenges during Rat, Dragon, and Monkey years, when good things are supposed to happen. Although the reverses are true too, there is no specific pattern. The 2004 Wood Monkey year was my stellar year. On February 8, 2005 I remember sitting at home and thinking darn, my great year is over and I will not have another one begin until February 1, 2024 when the year of the Wood Dragon begins. Then I thought of my niece, who is a Metal Snake born in 2001, so she was just beginning her stellar year and does not even know it. Then I thought how silly the whole thing is. The idea of only having a stellar year every 20 years and the first one is when you are four years old when you don't know it is ridiculous (hopefully every year of childhood is a stellar year). How about this, you believe in the astrology when it says you have a good year but discount it when it says you have a bad year. The reality is that we make our own fortune

What You Can Do

Some of you might be wondering what is the point of memorizing astrology? I found it interesting because it has dates, and to some degree, psychology. For example, why are the traits of certain signs compatible with the traits of certain other signs?. One way you can expand your memory is by memorizing information about a subject that is close to one you are already interested in. For example, if you are interested in the history of Broadway musicals, maybe you could additionally memorize the history of Greek Theater or Opera. If you like American History you could also learn European or Asian History. If you memorize enough about anything you will start to find it intriguing.

10

The Dark Side

Remembering everything that happened in my life and what day it happened on has one drawback. Not only do I remember the events but also I can reconstruct the exact emotions I was feeling. Initially, this might seem like a good thing because I have more happy memories than most people. However, the down side is that I have more unhappy memories than other people. People have a tendency to move away from pain and towards pleasure, so they tend to forget the unpleasant things. The 1975 hit song "The Way We Were" tells about forgetting painful things. Most people do choose to forget episodes which they have attached strong unhappy feelings. However, with my compartmentalized memories I have included every day for the past 40 years, and the emotions I have attached to them as if they are happening now. Sometimes this has made life seem heavy and burdensome. On any day of the year I tended to remember everything that happened on that day. I will take a day of the year and give examples.

December 30.

1970—Holiday trip to grandparents.

1971—Seeing the original Charlie and the Chocolate Factory at the movies

1973—Having a fit at home as only a 13 year old can have a fit.

1975—A holiday trip to my aunt's when I could not eat anything due to stomach upset.

1976—Trip to Center City Philadelphia.

1978—An annoying night at work in a Bagel Restaurant. I swore I needed to find another job.

1979—A nice trip to the Philadelphia Zoo. We saw the gorilla Massa on his 50th birthday. He had his back towards us the whole time.

1980—81—Nice visits to a lady friend's house.

1982—Fired from my first job as a college graduate, the job was as an aid on an adolescent unit in a psychiatric hospital, after I had been told twice that they were going to keep me. The shift supervisor had the nerve to say, "You can either hate us or appreciate the experience we gave you". This was followed by some visits to lawyer's offices that were no help in starting a lawsuit.

1989—I went to a nice party and had a lot of fun.

1998—A farewell luncheon for a coworker.

2003—Talked with some people about becoming a private contractor doing some counseling.

So, as you can see good and bad things happen to everyone on every day of the year. most people forget the bad, or at least they don't remember what date it was. For years I tended to make notes of what happened on each day, and then go about my business. On days, which were the anniversary of a significant event, I would remember it all day, ouch!

Having training in psychology and therapy I eventually found ways to cope with all this. I used a cognitive approach to change the way I thought about the event. For example, I decided to make December 30 a day that I would feel gratitude for having a job. And be grateful that 1978 and 1982 are history.

In recent years I have found another way to get over the memories, which stuck in my mind like doo on a shoe. I simply noticed the feelings, that the only reality is my having the feelings, and I can let go. So I just release on it. Learning this technique has helped me get rid of a plethora of sad and angry feelings from the past. For a year I reviewed everything that happened on that date and release all of the remaining unwanted feelings

For example:

September 23rd—1976 the time my driver—ed teacher yelled at me for slamming the brakes too hard.

1984—The night a young lady that I had dated twice said, "I don't see a chemistry".

1998—The day I missed teaching a college course due to a traffic jam on the expressway.

When I woke up on September 23 of the year I was doing this I would sit with the feelings one at a time.

1976—Feeling clammed up and angry.

1984—hurt, angry, and judgmental of the young lady.

1998—Embarrassed.

I would take each of these feelings, let myself feel them, realize that it is not the event, it's my making myself feel that way, and let it go. I am still working on this with an additional method, which involves tapping the meridians of the different nerves while you feel, the feeling. Using these methods, I am eliminating the dark side of having a good memory.

What You Can Do

Emotional charge is one factor, which increases the chance that you will remember something. You are more likely to remember an event that you were very happy about than an event, which you have no feelings about. However, some people remember an event that they experienced a strong unhappy feeling. Events when you felt sad, angry, afraid, depressed, or embarrassed about can stay with you. There is evolutionary significance to this. All unhappy emotions tell you that something is wrong and, deep down; all negative emotions make you feel that your survival is threatened. Let's take an example, suppose your boss at work tells you that they want to see you. Immediately you become tight in the stomach and anticipate losing you job, which could ultimately mean death, the income from you job sustains you. Then your higher brain, the neocortex takes over and tells you that you may not lose your job; the boss may just need to ask you about something. Even if you did lose your job you could find another one and collect unemployment until you do. Suddenly you no longer feel so uptight about the meeting.

Similarly you may recall a past incident in your life and still feel the same fear and upset about it as if it were happening now, even though it happened 20 years ago or more and is irrelevant to the circumstances of your present life. When you think of the incident you can tell yourself that it is no longer necessary to feel sad, angry, or fearful and there is no need to dwell on the negative past. As mentioned earlier in the chapter most people have a natural propensity to forget the bad and only remember the good, but if this is hard for you understand that it is just not necessary to hold on to negative emotion. You can let go.

11

Creative Thinking

There is one trick to my memory that people would not think of as a memory-enhancing tool. That is thinking outside the box. This expression is often used in business circles to mean thinking creative ideas to enhance productivity. However, there is a way to use it in your everyday life to enhance your memory and to make life more interesting.

Many people, as they are growing up, formulate their ideas and beliefs about how things are. After their late teens or early twenties they never revise them to fit new experiences. Suppose you believe that all people with high I.Q.'s are computer geeks or mad scientists, and are not athletic. Then you hear about a top student graduating at a top university who is starting at Microsoft for $100,000 a year. Another one is starting at a top pharmaceutical research lab. A third top graduate has decided to try out for an AAA level baseball team because he has a chance at making the majors. With your beliefs, you would probably pay more attention to the first two stories. You would not even remember the third story because it does not fit your belief system.

Similarly, suppose you are in high school and you have the belief that happiness is just for good-looking people. You know how happy the homecoming queen is at your school, and the George Clooney look alike who has the lead role in your school show. Then one day you are at your after school job in the local pharmacy. A short bald man with a limp walks in. You overhear him joking with some other customers and your coworkers. As you routinely register his purchases at the counter you routinely say, "Have a good day". Whereupon he smiles and says, "Never had a bad one". With your beliefs you will probably be taken aback, maybe think he is weird and quickly forget the entire exchange. Why? You perceive him as homely, but he seems to be happy.

I was always fortunate enough to never become enslaved by stereotyped thinking. When I met someone I would just observe everything about him or her but not make any assumptions. Then when I talked to them I would remember everything they said. Being this keen of an observer of people I noticed that stereotypes were often silly and wrong. People not only come in all different shapes and sizes, but all kinds of combinations of talents and interests. Someone could be good at both sports and music. Someone else might be solely dedicated to designing racetracks, or video games. When you take in all the information about someone there is no stereotype, just the information. Of course, I would link all information about a person together using the aforementioned techniques from previous chapters, but I would not ignore anything.

I found that keeping an open mind and not making assumptions is also a great way to make life more interesting. Most people lose their fascination with life when they lock themselves into their views and do not leave room for new learning. If there is one single way to make life more interesting it is to go around like the Curious Martian. Whenever you meet someone new or are learning something don't make any assumptions. Just take in the information. You will find that you have recovered the fascination with life that you had as a child, plus you will remember more.

12

A Means of Entertainment Who Needs American Idol?

The first time I thought of displaying my memory skills as a means of entertainment came when I was 13 years old. We were at the dinner table on Sunday October 14, 1973, and my parents were debating what date something had occurred on. I interjected that it was a Monday, and they looked at me with a deer in the headlights expression. Then my mom said, "Of course you would know". Whereupon the others started asking me when dates fell. Everyone seemed to be enjoying the game and I began wondering why television and radio exists. Years later when I was featured in the local paper for knowing dates my 84-year-old grandmother said, "All those silly singers and dancers they put on T.V., They ought to put you on".

Several months went by. It was now Friday May 31, 1974, and my schoolteachers decided there was to be a talent show on the last day of school. My music teacher was in charge so we had the privilege of watching some of the tryouts during our class time. I personally was very impressed with all the singing talent we had at our school (and I may add, a bit jealous). First we heard a young man sing "Nights in White Satin" and "American Pie". He was good. Then a seventh grade girl did an unforgettable rendition of "Sunshine on My Shoulder" Then two boys came in and did some magic. The boy came on and said "Ladies and Gentlemen, here is the amazing (a pause) then we hear an annoyed voice say "Red stone, idiot", Then the mascot yelled with enthusiasm "Red stone Idiot". As a 14 year old I thought that was hilarious. It is funny how easily young people are entertained.

Finally, a big ninth grader came out with his rock band (An electric guitar player) and belted out a song called "When I was Young" I think he wrote it himself. It was the kind of performance that Simon would say, "You are a star, and you are going to Hollywood"

While all these amazing performances were going on. I sat in my seat feeling like I was going to jump out of my skin. I thought of my encore performance at the dinner table a few months earlier and wondered if singing, magic, and dancing were the only accepted venues for this show, or whether I could get on stage and amaze people with my memory skills.

For several days I tried to muster enough courage to ask the music teacher for an audition. Finally on Wednesday June 5 I went to the music room after school and told my music teacher about my unique talent. For some reason, this was scary to do, and I had knots in my stomach for an hour before and during the revelation. It is amazing I did not stumble on my words. The nervousness was probably due to my never having told anyone outside of the family about my special talent, therefore I was unsure how others would react. Nevertheless, he gave me an audition.

The next day I got on the stage, lined up a row of my schoolmates. I asked them their birth dates and was, of course, able to tell them the day of the week they were born on. There was a pair of twins in the group who were soccer stars. I told them their birth date, Tuesday September 1, 1959 was during the Pan American Games in Chicago. So it is no wonder they were star athletes. I then told a friend of mine whose birthday is January 8 that he has the same birthday as Elvis Presley, and he said, "That is where I get my musical talent". Through this experience I learned to include little ditty's when I tell people their dates, so it evolved into an act of it's own

You can probably imagine how quickly the news of my phenomenal memory spread around the school. In Junior High if a boy and girl are seen talking to each other in study hall the romantic rumors fly. So you can imagine when it is revealed that someone has a phenomenal memory how quickly everyone would know. In every class my fellow students (This was the Nixon era "My fellow Americans") would tell the teacher to ask me some dates. When they told my history teacher he promptly left the room and ran downstairs to tell the principle and the guidance counselor about my special ability. At lunch every kid came up to me to ask me his or her birthday. The cafeteria became so unruly that the lunch proctor came up and tried to get everyone back to his or her seat. Two of my schoolmates grabbed me by each arm and led me to him, explained my memory. He asked me a couple of dates and said, "Take him away".

As the day wore on many of the boys offered to assist me in the act. They came up with names for my act such as "The Memory Wizard" and "Amazing Frank". One schoolmate who had not done a lick of schoolwork the entire year suddenly claimed he had the calendar memorized for the first week in June 1974. He then presented me with a piece of paper stating he and his friend would be my agents, and we would go on the road and perform. When I opened the paper it stated that he and his friend would get all the money from Amazing Frank. Boys will be boys.

Besides all the craziness of the day, I overheard some schoolmates discussing whether I could make a living doing this. Some of that went to my head, and for many years I would allow myself some grandiose fantasies about making millions entertaining people and never having to go to an office everyday. I had the first million spent on a beachfront shore house, a boat, a private plane, a limousine and chauffer to drive all my future dates and I all over the most exotic places in the world, London, Paris, Tokyo, Hong Kong, Miami. I imagined being honored by presidents and world leaders for my phenomenal expansion of the possibilities of human potential. I won the Nobel Prize for my contributions to Psychology and Education, Ding Dong, time for Algebra Class.

Monday June 10 was the eve of the talent show. I was on stage practicing with all my lackeys (about 123 schoolmates offered to help, okay maybe 10. They offered because they could get out of class for doing this). Suddenly during my rehearsal the vice principle of the school appeared. Apparently he did not share the enthusiasm that the music teacher and my schoolmates had for my performing. He asked me if I was willing to risk the probability of the rowdier kids making sarcastic remarks and shooting rubber bands and paper clips while I was on stage. I told him I did not think that would happen. However, he used the authority invested in him as the vice principal to expel me from the program. Perhaps surprisingly I was not disappointed. I do not get discouraged easily and I was proud to be given exposure. Even if one man thought a memory performance would not work for 12—14 year olds, maybe it would work for a mature audience.

In high school and college I always felt that my memory was something I could fall back on if another career did not materialize. Throughout the late 70s and early 80's there was a growing number of college graduates who were unemployed or under employed? Everyone talked about how bad the economy was and how hard jobs were to get. This caused me to think of some creative ideas in case I did not get a job becoming of my education.

The first idea was the one that was birthed with the talent show. I figured I would create a specific act and perform it for people. Like magicians and comedians I could perform at clubs, parties, etc.

Another idea was to memorize the directions to every business in Philadelphia and the surrounding areas, or as they said in those days, the burbs. I would include the details of what services they provided to a greater degree than the yellow pages provided. I could memorize the entertainment venues of clubs, theatres, the casinos etc. Then I would have a hotline where people could call to get information. My hotline would be financed by businesses that would pay me the money they would save on advertising. This was 1982 before most people had personal computers in their homes where they could go on a website or Expedia.com.

The third idea was to consult with firms about specific dates. I could give them specific information on the weather, conditions of the stock market. Etc.

These ideas provided an emotional security blanket in case everything else failed. However, I never had trouble obtaining employment. It was similar to the way some college-educated men learn basic construction, so if they get downsized they can do private contracting work. I am not belittling construction work here. I just feel that everyone should have more than one skill.

My interest in doing something with my special skill was rekindled in late 1988 when the movie "The Rain Man" came to theatres. It was about an autistic savant man who knew the calendar, the telephone directory, counting toothpicks and many other types of very useful information. When I saw the movie on Thursday December 29, 1988 I felt the same pang that I had felt watching the talent show tryouts half my life ago. Figuring that this was the best time to market my talent I immediately wrote letters to television stations, radio stations, and colleges where they do research on memory. I did get an article published in my local paper. Since more people now knew of my skill, I received occasional invitations to perform at parties. It was a great deal. I would spend about an hour answering people's questions about dates for a small fee. Then I could spend the rest of the time socializing and enjoying the party. Talk about a win win situation.

Here is a special note to all you brainiac boys and men who think you will never get the girl unless you are muscular, mean, or rich. I have found that when women learn of my memory skills they are not only impressed but many of them are attracted. Although I am still working on marriage, many of the women I have had were attracted to me because of my intelligence. As mentioned in a previous chapter I was not particularly athletic, I am not cocky or obnoxious, I actually have a very non-threatening accepting demeanor. So take heart all you brainy men. If you go into a nightclub or bar these days many of the women are wearing glasses that make them look smart. The kind that people used to say makes them look like a library lady. Boys and men today like a smart lady, and the corollary is true too, many women now like a smart man.

Even though I got a Masters Degree in Counseling Psychology, I could not get away from entertaining people with my memory skills. On the night I graduated with my degree my parents took me out to dinner in the restaurant where my brother was a bartender. The owner was this big tough German immigrant man named Klaus Rieneke. My brother introduced him to the family and explained my memory to him. With his thick German accent he said his father was born on April 20 and all German babies born in May of that year had the same father. I quickly figured out that all those Germans were honorary sons of Hitler (a strange thing to be telling people). On to a lighter note, he went around the restaurant asking customers their birth dates and coming back to me. Then I would tell him the date, despite having had a few drinks, and he would go yell to the restaurant "He said it was a Tuesday" etc. I enjoyed showing off and wished I had arranged a fee for entertainment.

Around the same time in the spring of 1991 I was commissioned to teach a course on memory. This was from Dr. Yvonne Kaye who wrote the book Cash and Codependency. She wanted to have an agency where people could have all kinds of support groups and self-improvement classes. My first class included a minister who wanted to improve his ability to remember the names and information about his parishioners It included a man who makes reservations for Amtrak, he wanted to be able to keep in his head some information as he was being bombarded with telephone calls of people making reservations, so he would not have to write as much. It was rewarding helping these people improve their skills. However, the most rewarding aspect of teaching memory was helping brain injured people regain their skills. In one class that I taught at the local school I had a young lady who had been brain injured in a car accident just six weeks earlier. During the first class she seemed unable to concentrate long enough to speak a complete sentence. By the time the class ended five weeks later she was applying what I taught and claimed she had almost completely regained her capacity. I had similar results with a 65 year old woman who had suffered asphyxiation in her attic a few months earlier on a hot day. Her brain had been without sufficient oxygen for several minutes before the paramedic arrived. Several months later I had her using my own brand of mnemonic techniques.

I discovered an additional way to use my skills in 2005 when my neighbor asked me to help her with her genealogy. She had all the dates of significant births and deaths in her family, and she wanted to know the day of the week of each date. Apparently the going rate for doing dates on a genealogy is $3.00 per date. So after one hour I had $511.00 in my pocket. Later that summer they ran a front-page article about me in the Atlantic City Press. I remember thinking that of all papers to have an article about my memory. I will never be allowed in a casino. Nevertheless about a month after I ran the article I gave a talk on memory for the Atlantic County Kiwanis. As I walked through the casino I realized I was wearing the same clothes that I wore in the newspaper photograph. As I walked past the blackjack tables I wondered what would happen if I just started playing. Would the people upstairs with the cameras recognize me instantly and eject me. I fought the temptation to find out.

What You Can Do

Telling people what day of the week they were born on and what the news and weather were certainly does not fall into the venue of typical entertainment. Then again all entertainment must have something atypical and interesting to hold the audiences attention. Essentially there are an infinite number of ways to entertain people; you just need to be creative and think of one. One Sunday November 21, 1993 I was on a day trip to the Baltimore Harbor. After touring the aquarium and some museums my friend and I were walking along the promenade at sunset. We saw a group of people lined up at a telescope. The person was charging a dollar a minute to look through and see Saturn. A man on stilts performs regularly on the boardwalk where I live in Ocean City New Jersey, and a woman I met at a party years ago does underdog routines at parades. Essentially the only requirement for something to be entertaining is for it to be out of the ordinary day to day experience of people. I would not recommend anything degrading just to get people's attention, such as wearing padding and charging people a dollar to kick you after a frustrating day at work. Anything that amuses people and is enjoyable for the performer is good entertainment.

13

More Mental Gymnastics

On November 19,1999 the news had a teaser for people. What is significant about the setup of that date? On the later editions of the news they
revealed that it would be the last date in over a thousand years that had all
odd digits in it. 11/19/1999. If November had 31 days in it the date
would have been the 31st. Then December does not count because it has
12 in it as the 12th month. . Of course, for the long interval between the
dates you have to include all four digits in the year. Otherwise the next
date would be November 11, 2011, 11/11/11. Then if you include the 0
in front of January through September 01 through 09 then November is
the only month of the year that can have all odd digits. October would be
10 and December 12. You can't have all odd digits for the entire third millennium because of the 2. Then you can't have it for the first century of
the fourth millennium because it would be 3000 something. . Then the
first decade and year of the second century would be 3100 to 3110. Finally
in 3111 you get to November and on the 11th you have all the odd. So
that is a hiatus of one thousand, one hundred eleven years and three hundred and fifty seven days without an odd digit in it.

Then less than three months later there was February 2, 2000, the first
date with all even digits in it 02/02/2000. This was the first date with all
even digits in it since August 28, 888. Since the entire second millennium
had a one in it 1000 through 1999. Then the final decade of the first millennium was 900 to 999. Then 889 to 899 had nines you go to 888. Then
September through December had 9,10,11, and 12 for the respective
months. Then August 29 through 31 had nines and threes, it falls to 08/
28/888. Interestingly the difference between the years is the same 112
years. The only difference is the number of days. The hiatus of all even

days is one thousand, one hundred eleven years and one hundred and fifty eight days. So it appears that dates with all even in them are slightly easier to come by than odd.

Another thing that I found interesting was when are the quarter marks, half marks, and three quarter marks of years. It would seem obvious that the middle of a calendar year would be June 30 going into July 1 at midnight. The three quarter mark would be September 30 at midnight, and the quarter mark would be midnight on March 31 going into April 1. Well, April fools, that is just not quite accurate.

A common year that has 365 days in it actually has 52 weeks plus one day, and a leap year has 52 weeks plus two days. For example January 1, 2007 will be a Monday but so will December 31, 2007. Then January 1, 2008 will be a Tuesday, but December 31, 2008 will be a Wednesday since 2008 is a leap year. If you compute the points of the year it would go as follows.

Since 2007 begins on a Monday and ends on a Monday, and has an even number of weeks in it the middle of the year would have to be at 12:00 noon on a Monday. This is because it begins at midnight Sunday going into Monday, and ends at 12 midnight on a Monday going into a Tuesday. June 30 going into July 1 will be a Saturday going into Sunday. So the actual middle of the year was 12 noon on Monday July 2. October 1 was a Monday, so the three quarter point of the year was 6P.M. on October 1. Then the quarter point of the year was 6 A.M. on Monday April 2.

Leap years follow a different system. 2008 begins at midnight on a Monday—Tuesday, and ends at midnight on a Wednesday-Thursday. So the half mark will be at midnight on Tuesday July 1 going into Wednesday July 2. The three quarter mark will be 12 noon on Wednesday October 1, and the quarter mark will be at 12 noon on Tuesday April 1. They say that April Fools Day began when some Europeans celebrated the New Year on April 1 instead of January 1. As you can see they only get the quarter point of the year right only on leap years.

If this was difficult to follow a diagram might help:

	Begins	one quarter	half	three quarters	ends
2007	12 A.M. Mon.	6A.M. Mon.	12 noon Mon.	6P.M. Mon.	12A.M. Tue
	Jan. 1	April 2	July 2	October 1	Jan. 1
2008	12 A.M. Tue	12 noon Tues	12A.M. Wed	12 noon Wed	12A.M. Thu
	Jan. 1	April 1	July 2	October 1	Jan. 1

Please note that I am not the only person in the world who makes a big hairy deal about number combinations. I remember on July 7, 1977 everyone was considering it the luckiest day of the century, since it had four sevens in the combination, like no other day, 7/7/77. On the news they interviewed people and whether they considered it lucky. I remember they had someone who had won a little bit of money in the lottery, and someone who failed to be hired for a job. These were typical things that could happen on any day. My thought was that the only thing lucky about it was that the casinos had not yet opened in Atlantic City, so they would not be swarmed with superstitious people losing their money.

Then, in the months leading to Y2K there was the 9/9/99 computer bug that never happened. Yes, we really needed another threat to our computers and the functioning of our society a short time before the fear of Y2K.

What You Can Do

It is somewhat enigmatic that I never developed an interest in doing crossword puzzles or playing video games. Although my generation was before the first one to have Game Boys and Atari sets all over the house, I considered games of that sort a frivolous waste of your time and mind. Yet I do all these mental gymnastics all the time. Doing puzzles and solving math problems and playing games does increase your mind power, provided there is thinking involved and not just manipulating a joy stick. It is generally believed now that when you learn a new skill you are creating neural pathways that increase your ability to perform many functions. You learn some mathematics it could also improve your creativity. You learn a new recipe it could increase your ability to learn a new dance step or instrument. All brain functions are interrelated.

14

Our Brains Are Like Computer Search Engines

Most of us have had the experience of using a computer search engine. You type the topic, press the arrow and are flooded with thousands and sometimes millions of sites. Many of the sites are only remotely related to the topic you are searching for. For example, you might be looking for information on jackhammers and get the website of every person named Jack. Our brains can work in a similar way. Here is a recent example of some things I linked together under the subtitle Los Angeles.

On Thursday March 1, 2007 I was on a plane heading for Los Angeles for the first time in my life. The two passengers beside me were asleep and I was not intrigued by the movie they were showing. In fact I was so disinterested that I do not even remember what it was. So I began linking up in my mind every association I could make with Los Angeles.

First I thought of obvious connections, City of Angels—then I thought of the song City of Angels. Then, while on the subject of songs I thought of Midnight Train to Georgia in which the first two words are L.A. Then I went into sports. There was the 1973 Super Bowl in which the Miami Dolphins defeated the Washington Redskins 14–3 and completed their perfect season. Then there was the play where the Miami kicker Garo Yepremian had a blocked kick and he picked up the ball and tried to throw a pass. What does this have to do with L. A? The game was played in the Coliseum. Then I thought of the 1984 Summer Olympics that were held in L.A. There were the Gymnasts Mary Lou Retton and Mitch Gaylord, the boxers Meldrick Taylor and Paul Gonzales, the track stare Carl Lewis, Roger Kingdom, and Edwin Moses. There was the British track star

Our Brains Are Like Computer Search Engines 81

Daliey Thompson who won his second out of three decathlons, and the 37 year old Carlos Lopez of Portugal who won the men's marathon. There were the swimmers Tracy Calkins and Nancy Hogshead. Then there was the laser show at the closing ceremonies.

Now I had all these facts associated with Los Angeles. Then I took it a step further and though of songs that were hits during the summer of 1984. There was the theme from the movie "Ghostbusters", and there was "Leave a Tender Moment Alone" by Billy Joel.

These songs have nothing to do with L.A. but I now associated them with L.A. because they happened to be hits at the same time that the Olympics were happening in L.A. Finally, I thought of a humorous song that was all about L.A. Sheryl Crowe's 1994 hit "All I Wanna Do", about crazy happenings in a bar which caused the bartender to be reading want ads.

Remember in a previous chapter on the moon landings I created a tree of associations which I added to as more moon landings took place, more moon landings, Then decades later I created a new branch when the movie Apollo 13 was made. I will now make a tree of associations with the Los Angeles information to illustrate how one can create associations which did not exist before.

Sports	Los Angeles—music	
	Summer 1984	*City of Angels*
1973 Super Bowl	Olympics	All I Wanna Do
Miami Dolphins 14	Mary Lou Retton	*Midnight Train to Georgia*
Washington Redskins 3	Mitch Gaylord	
Garo Yepremian	Carl Lewis	
Coleseum	Roger Kingdom	
	Edwin Moses	
	Dailey Thompson	
	Carlos Perez	
	Tracy Calkins	

Nancy Hogshead

Music

Ghostbusters

Leave A Tender Moment
Alone

It can be seen from this that every one of these facts I now associate with Los Angeles. The two songs at the bottom are the farthest removed, as their only connection to L.A is that they were hits during the Olympics. However, this is an illustration of how you can associate one thing to another until you have associated seemingly irrelevant facts to each other, and now it is easy to remember them.

What You Can Do

Try associating the following bits of information together

1988—Whitney Houston, Seoul South Korea, Boston Harbor, Donna Rice.

2000—Millennium, Y2K, Dade County, George Bush, Al Gore, Sandra Day O Connor, Derek Jeeter, Dante Culpepper, Élan Gonzales, Al Gore, The Perfect Storm, Scary Movie.

15

100 years, 112 palindromes

Within each century there is one palindrome year the most recent have been 1661, 1771, 1881, 1991, and 2002. They occur every 110 years except when it is a new millennium, and then it is only 11 years.

Palindrome days are much easier to come by, if you exclude the first two digits of the year when you write the date ex. 10/1/06 instead of 10/01/2006 they occur every 13 months and one day. For example, the palindrome days in the 1980's and 1990's were as follows.

January 8, 1981—1/8/81	January 9, 1991—1/9/91
February 8, 1982—2/8/82	February 9, 1992—2/9/1992
March 8, 1983—3/8/83	March 9, 1993—3/9/93
April 8, 1984—4/8/84	April 9, 1994—4/9/94
May 8, 1985—5/8/85	May 9, 1995—5/9/95
June 8, 1986—6/8/86	June 9, 1996—6/9/96
July 8, 1987—7/8/87	July 9, 1997—7/9/97
August 8, 1988—8/8/88	August 8, 1998—8/9/98
September 8, 1989—9/8/89	September 9, 1999—9/9/99

Each decade that is not the first one in a century follows the same pattern. However, in decades that have 0 in the ten's digit, all of the palindrome days fall in the same month, October of 01. This is because there is no month that is the 0th month of the year, but October is the 10th month. Following are all the palindrome days for this decade.

October 1, 2001—10/1/01
October 2, 2001—10/2/01
October 3. 2001—10/3/01
October 4, 2001—10/4/01
October 5, 2001—10/5/01
October 6, 2001—10/6/01
October 7, 2001–10/7/01
October 8, 2001—10/8/01
October 9, 2001—10/9/01
October 11, 2001—10/11/01
October 22, 2001—10/22/01

These are the only palindrome dates in this decade. Even though 2002 is a palindrome year it has no palindrome dates in it. The next palindrome dates will be in 2011, which will have 13.

January 1, 2011—1/1/11
January 11, 2011—1/11/11

Then November of 2011 will have the same dates that October of 2001 had the first nine, then the 11th and the 22nd. 2021 will have January 2 1/2/21, and January 21 1/21/21. And it will have all the December dates, the first nine, the 11th and the 22nd. So it too will have 13 palindromes.

What this decade lacks in consistent palindromes it makes up for in stutter dates. Each year has one date, which is the identical number in all three columns as follows. If you include the o's in all columns.

January 1, 2001—01/01/01
February 2, 2002—02/02/02
March 3, 2003—03/03/03
April 4, 2004—04/04/04
May 5, 2005—05/05/05
June 6, 2006—06/06/06
July 7, 2007—07/07/07

August 8, 2008—08/08/08
September 9, 2009—09/09/09

You may recall recently that people were dreading June 6, 2006 because it was three sixes, which is the symbol for the devil in the book of revelation. I know one person who dealt with this by having a party. June 6, 2006 was a beautiful spring day where I was so I hope nobody stayed in bed all day. Then on July 7, 2007 people flocked to the casinos thinking it will be almost as lucky as 30 years earlier 7/7/07 three lucky 7's 7/7/77 four sevens.

While we are on the subject of Friday the 13ths I would like to share my list of accomplishments on Friday the 13ths. On March 13, 1970 I was promoted to a higher reading group at school. On June 13, 1975 I won the English award at graduation. On January 13, 1978 I was given a role in the school show. On July 13, 1984 I won the prize in a raffle at an Astronomy Club. On January 13, 1995 I had a near miss in my car as a train came barreling through. The signal was broken and the watchman stuck his hand out to stop right when I was on the tracks. I put the petal to the metal instead and avoided being killed. I guess one can use their quick thinking and common sense to avoid Friday the 13th travesties.

16

Quick Calculations

Here is a quick way to calculate what day of the week any birthday you have which is a multiple of four. All you need to do is know the day of the week you were born. For any multiple of four (since there will be the same number of February 29ths in between) you can calculate as follows:

4, 32, 60, 88—subtract two days
8,36,64,92—add three days
12,40,68,96—add one day
16,44,72,100—subtract one day
20,48,76—subtract three days
24,52,80—add two days
28,56,84—same day

For example, say that you were born on a Wednesday, you subtract two from Wednesday and it would be a Monday. Then you would turn eight on a Saturday, add three to Wednesday and so forth. Sunday comes after Saturday when you are adding and Saturday comes after Sunday if you are subtracting. This only works for multiples of four because with other numbers there could be a different number of February 29ths in between. This also shows that there can be discrepancies of a day with people's birthdays. Let's take someone born in 1979 and 1980 and when they will turn 30. Someone born on Wednesday April 11, 1979 will turn 30 on Saturday April 11, 2009. But someone born on Friday April 11, 1980 will turn 30 on Sunday April 11, 2010. So the person born in 1979 will actually be a day older than the person born in 1980 when they celebrate the big 30. How does this happen? It is because 1980 was a leap year and 2010 will not be a leap year. So the person born in 1979 will have had eight February 29ths in their life 80,84,88,92,96,00,04, and 08, Whereas the person born in 1980 will just have had seven. They were not yet born on February 29, 1980. Consequentially, in states where the driving age is 16 everyone will be the same age on their 16th birthday, since 16 is a multiple of four. However, in states where the driving age is 17 some teens might have to wait an extra day. Similarly 18 is not a multiple of four so some have to wait an extra day to be eligible to vote. I wonder if that is the real reason for the Florida discrepancies in the 2000 presidential election. Furthermore, 65 is not a multiple of four so maybe the retirement age should be 68.

17

It Didn't Make Me Obsessive Compulsive

With all the precision it takes to memorize information and do the mental gymnastics that I do. One would wonder what I am like when it comes to everyday things. Am I Obsessive Compulsive about putting everything in the same place? Do I follow an exact routine every day and every week? Does my living room look like the showroom at Macy's? Perhaps surprisingly I am not obsessive compulsive, or as the slang expression goes, anal. Nor am I a total slob who does not pay any attention to everyday things such as looking nice and keeping the house clean. I am actually average when it comes to doing everyday things. I have never been obsessed with clothes or making a good appearance. However, I do like to look good. I pay my bills in a reasonable amount of time but I have been a little late on occasion. My house always looks good when I entertain, but being a bachelor I do let it go a little when it is just going to be me in the house.

One time I was watching a morning program and they had the sloppiest college student in the country receiving his $10,000 reward. You could not see the floor as he had pizza boxes and empty soda cans from who knows when. I remember thinking that I could not live in that environment. Conversely I find people who have a conniption every time there is a speck of dust on anything, they become nervous and unable to relax and enjoy life. The only thing about my house that one might expect is that I frequently run out of shelf space for books. Occasionally I have had to take old books, which I already read to a local book swap.

So even though I am precise with remembering dates and facts, I do not fit any stereotype of someone who is smart or obsessive. Obsessive is defined as having recurrent thoughts, and Compulsive is defined as having behaviors which one feels they have to do even though logic would deem them unnecessary. I do think I have obsessive thoughts, which allow me to memorize so much. I will hold on to a thought a little longer than most people seem to. I have observed that often in a conversation someone will want to change topics faster than when I am ready to, because I want to continue thinking about the topic at hand and discussing it. Additionally I have observed that I can stay in a good mood for longer than most people. My mother used to say that I would never get bored, because I can just think of something funny and laugh about it for an hour or more. Mom was right. I do not bore easily. Boredom comes from having the thought that something else is better than what you are experiencing in the moment. I circumvent that problem by thinking about some information I am memorizing.

Despite having obsessions, I do not have compulsions. I mentioned before that I do not have to keep my car and house spotless all the time, and I do not need to do everything a certain way.

18

Super Advanced Mental Gymnastics

Recall from a previous chapter that I divided the possibilities the dates can fall on into seven septets. Now later, I decided to designate them into twenty-eight categories giving each septet a number from one to four, depending on how far the year was from the previous leap. The first year, beginning March 1 the day after February 29 would be the first, then the second, third, and the fourth would be the year leading to the next February 29. An example of recent and upcoming years is as follows.

1st 7th—Monday March 1, 2004 to Monday February 28, 2005
2nd 6th—Tuesday March 1, 2005 to Tuesday February 28, 2006
3rd 5th—Wednesday March 1, 2006 to Wednesday February 28, 2007
4th 4th—Thursday March 1, 2007 to Thursday February 28, 2008.
Friday February 29, 2008 Skip the third.
1st 2nd—Saturday March 1, 2008 to Saturday February 28, 2009
2nd 1st—Sunday March 1, 2009 to Sunday February 28, 2010
3rd 7th—Monday March 1, 2010 to Monday February 28, 2011
4th 6th—Tuesday March 1, 2011 to Tuesday February 28, 2012.

Making these further distinctions led me to quickly be able to calculate for centuries the date any date was or will be. All I had to do was go forward and back in multiples of 28. If it were a date in the future I would subtract 30, add 2 and keep going until I had the year closest to the present and know the composition of the year. Let's take an example far into the future. July 27, 2088, first subtract 30 2058 add 2 2060, so 2060 would be the same as 2088. Then do it again. 2060 minus 30 would be 2030, add 2 and it would be 2032. Then go back 30 and you get 2002, add two is 2004. 2004 was the seventh so July 27 was a Tuesday. So it will be a Tuesday in 2088.

I found it even easier to calculate by comparing every 100 years. From the 19th to 20th century the days go back one. So if I knew that July 27, 1988 was a Wednesday then 2088 would be a Tuesday. For the other three out of four century changes the dates go back 2 because of the omission of February 29 in the 00 years. So let's calculate those dates for several centuries.

July 27, 1988—Wednesday
July 27, 2088—Tuesday
July 27, 2188—Sunday
July 27, 2288—Friday
July 27, 2388—Wednesday

So with skipping two in three out of four centuries and one every fourth century it becomes the same every 400 years.

Let's calculate some famous dates centuries ago with this formula. Those of you who were around may recall that July 4, 1976 was a Sunday, so when was our nation born. With the formula above July 4, 1876 would have been a Tuesday. So then July 4, 1776 was a Thursday. How about the Bicentennial of the Constitution, September 17, 1987 was a Thursday, so in 1887 it would have been a Saturday, and in 1787 a Monday. Then there is the Bicentennial of our Presidency. Washington was sworn in on April 30, 1789. April 30, 1989 was a Sunday. So April 30, 1889 was a Tuesday, and April 30, 1789 would have been a Thursday. Since we are going backwards with this we add instead of subtract.

How about the last century change before the millennium. You recall that January 1, 2000 was a Saturday. However, it was before February 29, 2000 so the rule of two dates will still apply. Since we are going backwards in time we would add two days. So January 1, 1900 was a Monday.

Obviously to do these calculations you still need to know a plethora of dates as I do in order to do the calculations. However, it might be fun to get a copy of a calendar of this century or last and do some calculations for events that were in a different century.

Often when I do not have anything that I have to be thinking about I will do some mental gymnastics; this is why I am never bored. If I am sitting in a traffic jam or waiting in a line I will rehearse some information. I might think, wow, the last time I was in a jam on these highways was Saturday October 24, 1992. It was sunny and seasonal. We had just celebrated the 500-year anniversary of Columbus. Then when I run out of information about one month I will pick another month and recite in my head everything I know about that month. June of 1925, it was the hottest June in this area up to that point with a mean temperature average of 78.0. We reached 100 degrees on the 5th and 6th. June 5th being the earliest the temperature got up to 100 on any year. The actor Tony Curtis was born on Wednesday June 3, 1925. On Tuesday June 23 the government in Atlantic City declared that women could now be on the boardwalk without wearing stockings, I guess the heat influenced that administrative decision. And I am sure both the women and the men in Atlantic City were happy.

When I go to bed at night, instead of counting sheep I will often think about facts in a similar manner to what I do in traffic and lines. I will go through decades and think what was the hottest day, month, year, of that decade, or what was the rainiest day or the biggest snowstorm. Or I will pick a number between 20 and 82 and think of the last five or six months that it was the local temperature average. For example, 51 degrees, November 2006, April 1997, November 1994, October 1988, April 1988, November 1985.

It seems that I always have to do my trivia a little different from the way other trivia buffs do it. Someone who is into sports trivia might know the averages of all New York Yankee players from 1951 to 1973 or all World Series winners and losers. Although I know a lot of that I always seem to tie dates into it. Another bedtime trick is to go through the decades and think of which Phillies and Eagles teams were the best and worst. For.

Example Phillies 70's Best 1977 worst 1972 80's—best 1980 worst 1988 90's—best 1993 worst 1996. I could go on and on. The biggest baseball card collector in the country owns one of the offices I see clients in. The walls outside the medical offices are covered with paintings and baseball trivia pictures. One Saturday between seeing my own clients I was alone and I stood and looked at a picture of Shea Stadium that had Mets trivia with the dates of all significant events in their history. I memorized it in a matter of minutes. It might have taken me longer if it did not include dates.

Words and names do not come quite as easily as dates when I try to remember them. It helps if I have a date that I can associate something with. It is probable that since I have so many associations with each date I can easily find something to attach the new information to and make an association. For example, when I saw on the Mets poster that they were first incorporated on October 16, 1960 I thought of two people I know that were born on that date and imagined them sitting at a long table with the Mets logo above them on the wall. So that date stuck as the date the Mets were incorporated.

You may be wondering what is the point of thinking about dates and trivia all the time. Why bother knowing these dates when you can easily look it up on the Internet, or even some cell phones have a perpetual calendar in them. Personally, I think we rely too much on technology. I think that the average person today has a worse memory that the average person 50 or 100 years ago, because we have too much technology at out fingertips. Technology is great for storing information, speeding calculations, advertising, and communicating when there is no time for a meeting. It is good for bringing people together when there is a great physical distance. However, it does not help when we rely on it so much that we don't exercise our brains anymore. When you do some mental gymnastics and memorize information it keeps you sharp similar to the way physical exercise helps your muscles to stay strong and not atrophy. Most people are now aware that Alzheimer's can be prevented, by keeping your mind going. So that is why I do it, and I would recommend to everyone, even people who do not consider themselves smart to do puzzles, read, or something to keep you mind active and healthy.

19

Does All This Thinking Stress Me?

Despite the advantages of thinking and remembering there are times when I need to stop thinking about dates and trivia. It can feel like butterflies in the head instead of the stomach. In 1997 I was in transition, moving from Pennsylvania to New Jersey. Between early September and mid November my days during the week consisted of the following. I would get up and leave the house at 8:00 A.M. in order to get to my 10:00 class I was teaching on time. It was an almost two hour commute. Then I would drive for about ten miles to my studio where I would give a couple of massages. Then I would drive for an hour and a half back to Pennsylvania to work the evening shift in a psychiatric hospital from 4P.M. to midnight. Finally, I would have to find time for lesson plans. This was the most stressful daily routine I have ever been in. Occasionally I would start thinking about dates and weather and become annoyed.

Life should be a good balance. When I have an occasional day where I am thinking too much I try to find a balance by calling people on the phone, going out, listening to music, watching a movie or reading something light, such as a joke book or novel. It is natural for anyone to seek balance in his or her life. The corollary of this is when I have been exercising, listening to music, or socializing I get the urge to memorize something new.

There were other times when memorizing was a stress reliever. When I was a child and teenager I would review information in my head whenever I was in a situation that I was not comfortable to be in. It is no wonder that I did not master social skills until my teenage and young adult years.

Here was this little boy who when introduced to someone new would be noting what date he was meeting someone when he was supposed to be saying" Hello, pleased to meet you". I think I was just nervous about meeting people and my inner world of facts and information was a safe haven. When I first began memorizing I would accost people in a store or in a doctors waiting room and ask them their birthday and their name. Then I would write it down on my calendar when I got home. My goal was to fill the entire calendar with each date being someone's birthday. I expended on that through the years and now you can name any day of the year and I will know either a celebrity or someone I know personally who has that day for a birthday. I get a kick out of listening to the radio and the DJ announces celebrities whose birthday it is and I already know them.

Another time when I would be flooding my brain with dates was in gym class growing up. I have alluded to the fact that I was not as athletic as I wished I had been. So when we would be playing a game I would be reeling off facts and figures in my head, it relieved the fear that I would not play well. Sometimes this caused me to miss the ball from not paying attention, and other times it caused me to play well because I was no longer thinking about how I was doing, and it resulted in better play.

In my career in the human services there are often days when the stress is very high. A client might get hurt, or threaten suicide. When I would be working my attention was totally focused on the client. However, as soon as the crisis passed my immediate focus became trivia. So in this sense I still use trivia as a stress reliever.

Wednesday July 7, 1999. The past few days had been so hot that if you stood on the sidewalk the heat would envelope your legs. You probably could have fried eggs on the sidewalk. Heat tends to exacerbate people's moods so there is more road rage, more crime, and more negative side effects for people on medications. On this day I was responsible for taking a 52-year-old man with paranoid schizophrenia to his appointment to get a psychiatric evaluation for medication. The heat of the past few days seemed to have made him more confused, anxious, and paranoid than usual, and he expressed a desire to kill himself when we were riding to the place.

When we arrived he refused to go in when his name was called. He said he is not taking any medicine and will not talk to the doctor. The psychiatrist came out and wanted to make him sign a contract that he will take medicine. The client started screaming and saying he is not suicidal so he does not need the medicine. Whereupon the doctor, in a rather unprofessional manner said, "He should be on the chronic unit at Ancora" (the State hospital) the client then screamed, "No, I'll sign". My next step was to pick up the medicine, get him home, and get his guardian to have him take the first dose. On the way to the pharmacy he again started in on "I won't take the medicine". I reminded him that if he does not take it I would have to bring him to the hospital to be assessed for inpatient treatment. Finally, we got the medicine, got him home, and with much cajoling his guardian giving him the medicine.

You can imagine by that time my nerves were frazzled. It was hot; I had to deal with a difficult, confused, suicidal client, and a doctor using inappropriate threats to intimidate him into compliance. Now it was finally time to take a break.

As I drove out onto the main highway I noticed a store in the distance called Butts and Betts (Meaning it sold cigarettes and lottery tickets) I suddenly had a recollection of something.

On Sunday July 7, 1974, twenty-five years earlier, there was a little quip in the Sunday paper about a 91-year-old man who had now been going to the movies every day for the past 25 years. He was a retired autoworker who moved to Miami and followed the same routine every day. First he would go to the local restaurant, order the same breakfast every day then head for the theatre. So I had a flashback to that day when I was 14 years old and at the shore. I remember swimming in the ocean marveling about how this man had been going to that theater every day of my life and for eleven years before I was born. I chuckled at the idea that now I will not only be able to tell people the day of the week things happened but I can tell them something that happened in the world every day since Thursday July 7, 1949. I also questioned how Paul's life was otherwise. Did he do anything else? Was he not involved in a senior citizens group? Does he ever go to the beach? How often do they change features at that theater? (This was before the age of multiplexes; sometimes an inner city theater would show the same feature for months). Would he have died years ago if he did not have that to look forward to each day? Finally I decided that this was too deep for a 14-year-old boy at the shore on Independence Day Weekend to be thinking about, so I got involved with a bunch of kids who were throwing a tennis ball around in the water.

Now let's go Back to the Future, to 1999. I decided I just had to stop in Butts and Betts and get a paper. Let's see if Paul has now been going to the movies every day for the past 50 years and he is still alive and wolfing down that popcorn at age 116. Sadly, there was no feature in the paper. I then wondered when he died, maybe they just did not put it in, or maybe at least there is a multiplex there now so he would have more choices of movies to see. But then if they did that the theater would have had to close for several months while they re built it, then what would he do? Well, at any rate it provided some comic relief from the stressor of dealing with that client. Like a client with Obsessive Compulsive Disorder I just had to know if Paul Morgan was still hitting that Movie Theater, damn!

What You Can Do

When you really think about it. There are very few things you have to do in life, and you are permitted to think about whatever you want. Consequentially there are very few reasons to ever get stressed. It is healthy to daydream and think of something pleasant even in the middle of a stressful situation (provided it does not require your immediate attention) Even when you have to be concentrating on the stressor, as soon as you don't have to be you can find a way to distract and entertain yourself. Most people spend more time than they have to fretting over things that have not happened yet, or feeling stressed over an event that is over, or something that they can't do anything about it right now. Find your own unique way to redirect your mind after a stressful event, as I did.

20

More Tips for Developing your own Skills

Even if you don't care about celebrity birthdays and senior citizens movie dates, there are many ways that you can increase your own skills. I am sharing all the methods that I used from trial and error. This is because there are many books and tapes on the subject, and I do not want to steal anyone's ideas.

Basically, the first thing you need to do is be mentally present when you are learning the information. Whether you are in a class lecture, meeting someone for the first time, or reading the paper and want to retain what you learned. You need to get all distracting thoughts out of your head. Years ago I went to an experiential retreat for a weekend, then eight months later I went back to take a longer course. I was surprised at the number of staff and volunteers who remembered my name and a plethora of information about me. Additionally they seemed to have the same recollection of everyone who was there. Finally, one day I asked one of the staff members how they were able to have such great recollection of everyone. She said it is because we are focused and present, no other reason. So, the most basic rule of developing good memory is to get rid of all distracting thoughts and pay attention.

This is the reason why children seem to be able to remember almost everything. They have natural curiosity, and no one is telling them to censor anything. So they are like sponges and their knowledge is like the water. They take in everything with no pressure to learn it and no judgments about learning. So they just focus naturally and retain. So another trick to remembering is to recapture the childlike curiosity about everything. When someone is talking about a subject you know nothing about, just take it in and don't be thinking, "This is boring" or try to change the subject. When you see something on T.V. that you are unfamiliar with, watch and take it in. You will find you learned and remembered a lot.

Most people find that they have an easier time remembering information if it pertains to a subject they are interested in. Naturally it is easier to be focused and block out distracting thoughts when you are interested in the subject matter. So how do you do it if the subject is something boring?

The feeling of boredom comes when you are thinking that you would rather be doing something else. The trick is to identify what you would rather be doing and then tell yourself in your head that you will get to it later. Then relax and focus on the subject matter. Usually after you have focused on a subject for a few minutes it will become interesting, you would be surprised. Say you are an English major in college and you are sitting in a Biology lecture, because you have to take at least one science course to graduate. You would rather be analyzing Shakespeare, or Hester Prynn, but instead you are learning about the Krebs Cycle and the Calvin Cycle. You could use your creativity which attracted you to English in the first place, and make up a story about Calvin Krebs Cycle Shop, similar to the stories I shared in previous chapters. That will make it more interesting for you and make it easier to stay focused on the lecture. You may find that you no longer need to make up stories after some time, because you become naturally interested in biology.

One of the reasons I remember things is because I hold the thought for a longer period of time than most people seem to. When I want to remember something such as someone's name or a fact I think about it undistracted for at least five minutes. By that time it is registered in my long—term memory. It takes several minutes of undistracted thought for something to register in your long-term memory, and the longer you hold a thought the more interesting it will seem. It is just the way the mind works.

While I developed my memory by attaching everything to dates, you can start developing yours by attaching everything to a subject you are already interested in and have some knowledge of. Even if you are not an expert, if you have enough facts about a subject you can connect new information on any subject with the old information on your favorite subject.

Suppose you are a man who has a working knowledge of history and fishing. Then one day, for reasons you cannot fathom your wife decides to register you and she for square dancing lessons. You don't want to go but you agree to try it to keep the peace in the house. First you will learn the Virginia Reel, which includes a move called Do Se Do. To remember the name of the dance you could think of Virginia Dare, whom the state of Virginia was named after, imagine a woman whom you are about to lock arms with and spin around is Virginia and you are the fish that she is reeling in (No one will know you are thinking this, so your pride will be protected, plus if it is a different woman than your wife she won't know you are thinking you are being reeled in) Then you lock arms and make a circle, which is the do se do, Imagine you and she are pieces of dough you are using to make bread and you look at each other (dough seeing dough). By this time you will have made some amusing pictures and might be amusing yourself into enjoying the square dancing, and you don't even have to tell the guys at work you went and enjoyed it.

Another tip is to have a positive or even neutral attitude towards learning in general. If you are in school or learning things for a new job and you think. This is a lot of work and it's a pain you will experience difficulty in learning it and being motivated, and you will likely procrastinate if you think the memorizing is painful. If you are feeling relaxed and curious it will come more easily. One way to develop curiosity towards something is to ask questions, even if you do it in your head. Back to the question of the Calvin and Krebs Cycles, if you ask, why is that combination involved, and not another set of elements? By asking the question you will be making it interesting to you.

In a previous chapter I expressed the idea that when you learn something in one area of endeavor you increase your capacity to learn in other areas. They used to think that there was no compensation in the brain. Consequentially, if you took a walk and memorized the names of your neighbors and matched them with the street numbers on their mailboxes you would have increased your ability to match names with numbers but that would be it. Now it is known that if you go memorize you neighbor's addresses, then when you get inside you learn a new function on your new P.C. Then you leaf through a gardening book and visualize combinations of flowers and how they would look in your garden this year. Then you calculate the cost of the mulch, flowers, pots etc. Then you learn a new exercise routine, and then you cook a new dish. All of these new things you learn will augment each other and make the learning of each skill easier.

Now for the specifics of how to create the pictures of the visualizations, I will use an example from chapter 3 of Apollo 13 to Apollo 14.

1. Recite the information from rote ten times or more. This will prevent you from mixing words when your associations are not the same exact word as the thing you are associating it to. For example you picture an ailing shepherd on the moon ailing is not the same as Alan but close. So first repeat a few times "Apollo 14, Fra Mauro region, Alan Shepherd, Edgar Mitchell, Golf ball shot on the moon, February 5 and 6 1971".

2. Break information down into sections Apollo 14 is a section, Alan Shepherd is a section.

3. Take each section and create a picture. Apollo 14. The sun (Apollo was the sun god, with a flag that says 14 on it. Fra Mauro (Two people about to argue and get on each other's nerves, imagine the feelings, for Fray. Then they decide that they will postpone the fray until tomorrow Mauro) One of the people fighting is a shepherd who looks sickly, (ailing shepherd for Alan Shepherd) .The other has headgear on in case it gets cold and he might chill (Headgear Edgar, might chill Mitchell, feel the chill as you imagine this.). Suddenly Hank Aaron and Babe Ruth appear (If you look at the guide at the end of this chapter their birthdays are February 5th Aaron, and 6th Ruth) Babe Ruth decides to discard his bat for a golf club and the ailing shepherd joins him (Alan Shepherd shot a golf ball on the 6th)

4.   Create pictures of what it sounds like. I find it helpful to say the word a few times and I get different pictures from that. For example Edgar, Edgar Edgar, Head Gear. Mitchell, Mitchell, Mitchell, Might chill. Another way is to look at the spelling and break it apart. Often you can get two words and make an association from that. Mit—Might Chill—Chill.

5.   You repeat steps 2 through 4 with the new part of the information. We already did this in the example of step 3.

6.   When you create the pictures make them resemble movies rather than photographs or paintings. Motion works better than still. For example, imagine the action of hitting the golf ball as they follow through on their swing.

7.   Create a bridge to bring each piece of information together. In the step three example you have the two men postponing the fray, the descriptions of them are how we bridged Fra Mauro with Alan Shepherd and Edgar Mitchell. Let's create a bridge linking Apollo 14 with 13 and 15. At the beginning of the Apollo 14 section we could say that the fray was caused by the bad luck of 13 and it irritated the two men. For Apollo 15 we could say that after the golf ball shooting the ailing shepherd and headgear man leave as they see a moon rover vehicle coming with a sign of the sun and the number 15 on it. Then you will have connected it to both missions and continue the tree, as described in Chapter 3.

My own belief is that anyone can develop as good a memory as they want. So maybe you don't necessarily want to develop your skills to the extent that I have. However, you can develop the skills to achieve any goal that is important to you. Whether you are a biology student wanting to fare well enough to get into medical school, a minister wanting to learn the names and information about the parishioners in your new church, or a person with a head injury who would like to regain some capacity. You can learn using the techniques that I used to develop my memory. We can all do more than we think.

If you need to be able to remember numbers, you can make associations of the number to a person or something pictorial. I have a list here of celebrity birthdays for every day of the year. You can make two or three digit number associations for the date by picturing the celebrity, and then create a story for the longer numbers that combines celebrities.

January

1. Ellen Degenres, Paul Revere, Betsy Ross

2. Isaac Asimov

3. Mel Gibson, Victoria Principal

4. Jane Wyman

5. Diane Keaton

6. Danny Thomas

7. Nicholas Cage

8. Elvis Presley, David Bowie

9. Richard Nixon

10. Rod Stewart, Pat Benetar

11. Alexander Hamilton

12. Howard Stern, Kirstie Alley

13. Charles Nelson Reilly, Patrick Dempsey

14. Andy Rooney, Faye Dunaway

15. Martin Luther King

16. Ethel Merman, Ronnie Milsap

17. Benjamin Franklin, Muhummad Ali

18. Cary Grant, Kevin Coster

19. Janis Joplin, Dolly Parton, Desi Arnaz Jr.

20. George Burns

21. Telly Savalas

22. Bill Bixby, Linda Blair

23. Humphrey Bogart

24. Ernest Borgnine, Ray Stevens

25. W. Somerset Maugham

26. Paul Newman, General Douglas Macarthur

27. Wolfgang Ammadeus Mozart, Mikhail Barishnakov.

28. Alan Alda

29. Oprah Winfrey

30. Dick Martin, Phil Collins

31. Carol Channing

February

1. Victor Herbert

2. Farrah Fawcett

3. James Michener, Morgan Faichild

4. Charles Lindberg, David Brenner

5. Hank Aaron, Christopher Guest

6. Babe Ruth, Zsa Zsa Gabor

7. Charles Dickens

8. Ted Koppel, Jack Lemmon

9. Mia Farrow

10. Jimmy Durante, Robert Wagner

11. Thomas Edison, Burt Reynolds

12. Abraham Lincoln, Arsenio Hall

13. Tennessee Ford, Peter Tork

14. Jack Benny

15. Galilleo, Ceasar Romero

16. John Mc Enroe, Sonny Bono

17. Hal Holbrook

18. Yoko Ono, Cybil Sheppard

19. Smokey Robinson, Cass Elliott

20. Sydney Pontier, Gloria Vanderbilt

21. Erma Bombeck

22. George Washington, Drew Barrymore

23. Peter Fonda

24. James Farentino

25. George Harrison, Zeppo Marx.

26. Jackie Gleason, Tony Randall

27. Ralph Nader, Elizabeth Taylor

28. Zero Mostel

29. Anthony Robbins

March

1. Glenn Miller, Ron Howard

2. Dr. Seuss, Bon Jovi

3. Alexander Graham Bell, Jackie Joyner Kersee

4. Knute Rockne, Paula Prentiss

5. Rex Harrison, Andy Gibb

6. Ed McMahon

7. Tammy Faye Baker

8. Lynn Redgrave

9. Bobby Fisher, Jeffery Osborne, Buggsy

10. Chuck Norris

11. Lawrence Welk

12. Liza Minelli, James Taylor

13. Neil Sedaka

14. Albert Einstein, Billy Crystal

15. Andrew Jackson, Judd Hirsch

16. Jerry Lewis

17. Nat King Cole, Kurt Russell

18. Grover Cleveland, Wilson Pickett, Vanessa Williams

19. Glenn Close, Bruce Willis

20. Mr. Rogers, Spike Lee

21. Mathew Broderick, Rosie O' Donnell

22. Chico Marx, Andrew Lloyd Webber

23. Joan Crawford

24. Steve McQueen

25. Howard Cosell, Elton John

26. Leonard Nimoy, Diana Ross

27. Gloria Swanson, Mariah Carey

28. Reba Mc Entire

29. Pearl Bailey, Elle McPherson

30. Eric Clapton, Celine Dijon

31. Richard Kiley, Herb Alpert

April

1. Debbie Reynolds

2. Hans Christian Anderson

3. Marlon Brando, Eddie Murphy

4. Robert Downey Jr.

5. Bette Davis, Gregory Peck

6. Billy Dee Williams

7. David Frost, John Oates

8. Julian Lennon

9. Dennis Quaid

10. John Madden, Don Meredith

11. Louise Lasser

12. David Cassidy, Tiny Tim

13. Thomas Jefferson

14. Pete Rose

15. Leonardo Da Vinci

16. Kareem Abdul Jabbar

17. Harry Reasoner

18. Hayley Mills, Conant O'Brien

19. Dudley Moore.

20. Ryan O'Neill, Jessica Lange

21. Anthony Quinn, Tony Danza

22. Peter Frampton

23. William Shakespeare

24. Barbara Streisand

25. Edward R. Murrow, Al Pacino

26. John James Audobon

27. Ulyssees S. Grant

28. James Monroe

29. Jerry Seinfeld

30. Cloris Leachman, Willie Nelson

May

1. Judy Collins

2. Dr. Benjamin Spock, Bing Crosby

3. James Brown, Peter Gabriel

4. Audrey Hepburn

5. Tammy Wynette

6. Willie Mays

7. Johnny Unitas

8. Harry Truman

9. Billy Joel, Candice Bergen

10. Fred Astaire

11. Irving Berlin

12. Burt Bacharach, George Carlin

13. Stevie Wonder

14. Bobby Darin

15. Eddie Arnold

16. Henry Fonda, Liberache

17. Debra Winger

18. Pope John Paul 11, Perry Como

19. Pete Townsend

20. Joe Cocker, Cher

21. Raymond Burr, Leo Sayer, Me

22. Sir Lawrence Olivier

23. Joan Collins

24. Bob Dylan, Pricilla Presley

25. Robert Ludlam, Beverly Sills

26. Stevie Nicks

27. Henry Kissinger

28. Gladys Knight

29. Bob Hope

30. Benny Goodman, Wyonna Judd

31. Brooke Shields

June

1. Marilyn Monroe, Andy Griffith

2. Marvin Hamlisch

3. Tony Curtis, Jefferson Davis

4. Dennis Weaver, John Drew Barrymore

5. Robert Lansing

6. Levi Stubbs

7. Prince, Tom Jones

8. Joan Rivers, Johnny Depp

9. Michael J. Fox

10. Judy Garland

11. Gene Wilder

12. Jim Nabors, George Bush Sr.

13. Richard Thomas, Tim Allen

14. Boy George

15. Courtney Cox

16. Stan Laurel

17. Dean Martin, Barry Manilow

18. Paul Mc Cartney

19. Paula Abdul, Guy Lombardo

20. Cyndi Lauper

21. Juliette Lewis

22. Kris Kristofferson, Meryl Streep

23. June Carter Cash

24. Mick Fleetwood

25. Carly Simon, George Michael

26. Peter Lorrie, Chris O Donnell

27. Helen Keller

28. Henry VIII, Mel Brooks

29. Nelson Eddy

30. Buddy Rich, Florence Ballard

July

1. Princess Diana

2. Cheryl Ladd

3. Montel Williams

4. Geraldo Rivera, Abigail Van Buren, Ann Landers

5. Huey Lewis, P.T. Barnum

6. Sylvester Stallone, George W. Bush

7. Ringo Starr, Shelley Duvall

8. Steve Lawrence

9. O.J. Simpson, Fred Savage

10. Fred Gwynne,Arlo Guthrie

11. Yul Brynner, Selya Ward

12. Bill Cosby, Milton Berle

13. Harrison Ford

14. Rosey Grier

15. Linda Rondstandt, Forest Whitaker

16. Orville Redenbacher, Ginger Rogers

17. James Cagney, Luci Arnaz

18. Red Skelton

19. Richard Jordan, Vicki Carr

20. Natalie Wood

21. Robin Williams, Cat Stevens

22. Bobby Sherman, Danny Glover

23. Monica Lewinski

24. Lynda Carter

25. Walter Brennan

26. Mick Jagger

27. Norman Lear

28. Sally Struthers

29. Peter Jennings

30. Arnold Schwartzennager

31. Dean Cain

August

1. Jerry Garcia, Herman Mellville

2. Carroll O' Connor

3. Tony Bennett, Martin Sheen

4. Louis Armstrong

5. Loni Anderson

6. Lucille Ball, Andy Warhol

7. Billie Burke, B.J. Thomas

8. Dustin Hoffman, Esther Williams

9. Melanie Griffith, Whitney Houston

10. Eddie Fisher

11. Mike Douglas, Joe Jackson

12. Buck Owens

13. Alfred Hitchcock

14. David Crosby, Danielle Steel, Steve Martin

15. Napolean, Julia Child

16. Kathie Lee Gifford, Madonna

17. Sean Penn, Robert DeNiro

18. Robert Redford, Shelley Winters

19. Bill Clinton

20. Connie Chung

21. Kenny Rodgers, Count Basie

22. Ray Bradbury, Valerie Harper

23. Gene Kelly, Babara Eden.

24. Steve Guttenberg

25. Leonard Bernstein, Elvis Costello

26. Macauley Calkin

27. Tuesday Weld, Pee Wee Herman

28. David Soul

29. Michael Jackson, Richard Gere

30. John Phillips

31. Van Morrison, Debbie Gibson

September

1. Gloria Estefan, Conway Twitty.

2. Linda Pearl

3. Kitty Carlisle, Charlie Sheen

4. Paul Harvey, Mitzi Gaynor

5. Bob Newhart, Raquel Welch

6. Jane Curtin

7. Buddy Holly

8. Sid Ceasar, Patsy Cline

9. Otis Redding, Michael Keaton

10. Jose Feliciano

11. D. H. Lawrence, Harry Connack Jr.

12. Maurice Chavalier,

13. Jacqueline Bisset

14. Joey Hetherton

15. Robert Benchley, Agatha Christie, Oliver Stone

16. Lauren Becall, Peter Falk

17. Anne Bancroft

18. Greta Garbo, Frankie Avalon

19. Joan Lunden, Twiggy

20. Sophia Loren

21. Stephen King, Bill Murray

22. Debby Boone

23. Bruce Springsteen, Ray Charles

24. Jim Henson, F. Scott Fitzgerald

25. Christopher Reeve, Barbara Walters

26. Olivia Newton-John

27. Meat Loaf, Cheryl Tiegs

28. Ed Sullivan

29. Gene Autry, Bryant Gumbel

30. Johnny Mathis, Truman Capote

October

1. Jimmy Carter, Julie Andrews, Richard Harris, Walter Mathau

2. Groucho Marx, Tiffany

3. Chubby Checker, Gore Vidal

4. Patti Labelle, Charlton Heston

5. Allen Ludden

6. Shana Alexander, Britt Eckland

7. John Cougar Mellencamp

8. Chevy Chase

9. John Lennon, Jackson Browne

10. Tanya Tucker, Ben Vereen

11. Luke Perry, Daryl Hall

12. Luciano Pavaratti

13. Marie Osmond, Art Garfunkel

14. Dwight Eisenhower, William Penn

15. Sarah Ferguson, Lee Iacocca

16. Suzanne Somers

17. Evil Kneivel, Rita Hayworth

18. Jean Claude Van Damme, Chuck Berry

19. John Lithgow

20. Tom Petty, Dr. Joyce Brothers, Art Buchwald

21. Carrie Fisher, Manfred Mann

22. Christopher Lloyd

23. Johnny Carson

24. Kevin Kline

25. Pablo Picasso

26. Marla Maples

27. John Cleese

28. Charlie Daniels, Julia Roberts

29. Wyonna Ryder

30. Charles Atlas, Henry Winkler

31. Dan Rather, Michael Landon

November

1. Stephen Crane

2. Burt Lancaster

3. Charles Bronson, Roseann Barr

4. Walter Cronkite, Will Rogers

5. Tatum O'Neil

6. Sally Field

7. Johnny Rivers, Joni Mitchell

8. Billy Graham, Catherine Hepburn

9. Dr. Carl Sagan

10. Richard Burton, Mackenzie Phillips

11. Demi Moore, Leo DeCaprio

12. Neil Young, Grace Kelly

13. Whoopi Goldberg

14. Brian Keith, MacLean Stevenson

15. Ed Asner, Petrula Clark

16. Diana Krall

17. Danny Devito, Rock Hudson

18. George Gallup, Linda Evans

19. Larry King, Meg Ryan, Jodie Foster

20. Bo Derek

21. Harpo Marx, Marlo Thomas

22. Rodney Dangerfield, Jamie Lee Curtis

23. Boris Karlott

24. Scott Joplin

25. Robert Kennedy, John F. Kennedy Jr., Amy Grant

26. Charles Schulz, Tina Turner

27. Bruce Lee, Jimi Hendrix

28. Judd Nelson, Randy Newman

29. Dick Clark, Chuck Mangione

30. Mark Twain, Billy Idol

December

1. Woody Allen, Bette Midler, Lou Rawls

2. Brittney Spears

3. Ozzy Osborne, Andy Williams

4. Jeff Bridges

5. Walt Disney

6. Agnes Moorehead

7. Harry Chapin

8. Sammy Davis Jr., Jim Morrison

9. Donny Osmond, Kirk Douglas

10. Emily Dickinson

11. Jermaine Jackson

12. Frank Sinatra, Dionne Warwick

13. Dick Van Dyke

14. Lee Remick, Patty Duke

15. Tim Conway

16. Liv Ullman

17. Eugene Levy

18. Brad Pitt, Steven Speilberg

19. Jennifer Beals, Allyssa Milano

20. George Roy Hill

21. Phil Donahue, Frank Zappa

22. Diane Sawyer

23. Elizabeth Hartman

24. Howard Hughes, Ava Gardner

25. Jimmy Buffett, Sissy Spacek

26. Steve Allen, Phil Specter

27. Marlene Dietrich

28. Denzel Washington

29. Mary Tyler Moore, Ted Danson

30. Bo Diddley, Davey Jones, Michael Nesmith

31. John Denver, Donna Summer

With this knowledge, you can make a story for every set of numbers that you have to memorize. Let's suppose you are trying to remember someone' telephone number 205–362–7825. First, include the person in the story, Then associate them with Hank Aaron, because his birthday is February 5 or 2/5 or 205. You can imagine that person hitting a home run in a Braves uniform. Then as they round home plate they start laughing and holding up a check for $1,000,000 like Ed McMahon (March 6) or 36. Then they quick tuck the check away and say "Bah Humbug" like Scrooge, a Charles Dickens character February 7 or 27. Then a baton grows out of their hand and they start conducting a chorus in the stands singing "Life can be free in America" from West Side Story, a Leonard Bernstein production for 825. His birthday is August 25. So now you have your friend being Hank Aaron 205, Ed Mcmahon, 36 Charles Dickens, 27 and Leonard Bernstein 825. You have now memorized their telephone number by memorizing four birthdays.

Suppose you need to know the date and time of a dentist appointment you have. It is on April 25 at 3:30 P.M. First you can imagine the police-man Serpico cleaning your teeth (his birthday, Al Pacino who played him is April 25). There is musical entertainment there to ease the pain. Eric Clapton walks in to entertain you (his birthday is 330, March 30). So now, by visualizing celebrities doing your activities, or you doing their activities you will never even have to write anything down. It may seem difficult to do this at first but the more you practice, the better you will be and even find it easier than programming it into your cell phone.

Although I may be a highly intelligent person, I am not so intelligent that I can anticipate and imagine every need that you may have for mem-ory training. Therefore if you have any questions about material that you may need to memorize, please direct them to the website in the postscript.

This book was started on Wednesday June 8, 2005, and completed on Tuesday July 10, 2007

Afterword

Even though we now have the capacity to store our information in computer files, palm pilots, and even our cell phones, most people still have needs to memorize information. I am planning to publish a workbook that will be based on the requests of the readership. If you have some type of information that you need help with memorizing please send it to me in the following format.

1. Make a list of at least one thing that you are knowledgeable about. It could be history, auto mechanics, literature, sports, entertainment, or anything. You do not have to be an expert but just possess some knowledge and interest.

2. Indicate something that you need to memorize, but are having trouble with.

   You can send the inquiries to www.phenomenalmemory.com or to healysheal1@msn.com The most intriguing inquiries will appear in The workbook with an answer and the name of the person who inquired.

About the Author

Frank Healy is a life coach who specializes in improving your memory. He is a Licensed Professional Counselor in the State of New Jersey. He lives in Ocean City and is employed as a counselor at Cape Counseling and Associates for Life Enhancement. He teaches at Atlantic Cape Community College. Frank has designed and taught courses in how to improve your memory. This is his first book on the subject

Recourses

Berk, Laura. Infants, Children, and Adolescents, Allyn and Bacon, Boston, Mass. 5th Edition, 2004

Csikszentmikhalyi,Mihaley. Flow, The Psychology of Optimal Experience. Harper and Row Publishers, 1990

Daniel, Clifton, Editor in Chief, Chronicle of the 20th Century. Chronicle Publications, Mount Kisco, New York. Distributed in the United States by Prentice Hall, A Division Of Simon and Schuster, New York, New York. 1988

Davenport, Robert. The Celebrity Birthday Book. General Publishing Group, Santa Monica, California. 1996

Dwoskin, Hale. The Sedona Method. Sedona Press. Sedona, Arizona. 2003

Geiger, Peter, Chief Editor, and Duncan, Sondra, Managing Editor. Farmer's Almanac. Almanac Publishing, 185862, Lewiston, Maine 1998

Glover, Robert. No More Mr. Nice Guy. Running Press Book Publishers. Philadelphia, Pennsylvania 19103-4399

Historical Society of Pennsylvania. 1300 Locust St., Philadelphia, Pennsylvania, 19107

Lau, Theodora. Handbook of Chinese Horoscopes, Harper-Collins, New York, New York, 1996

Mason, Robert, Editor. Life in Space, Time-Life Books, New York, 1983

Life Magazine, July 1994 edition

The (Philadelphia) Sunday Bulletin. July 7, 1974

Alexandr RomanavichR Luria, Lynn Solotaroff,Translated Form The Russian. Forward by Jerome S. Bruner The Mind Of A Mnemonist, 1968 Harvard University Press, Cambridge Massachusetts and London England.

Langer, Ellen J. The Power of Mindful Learning, 1997, A Merloyd Lawrence Book, Addison-Wesley, Reading Massachusetts.

Wood, Samuel. Wood, Ellen Green. Boyd, Denise. Mastering the World of Psychology, Second Edition Pearson, 2006.

Websites

Emotional Freedom Techniques. www.emofree.com

History Channel, The. www.historychannel.com

NOAA Weather Archives. www.nws.noaa.gov

Philadelphia Eagles. www.philadelphiaeagles.com

Philadelphia Phillies. www.philadelphiaphillies.com

Wikepedia. En.wikepedia.org.

Tapes

O'Brien, Dominic. Quantum Memory Power, Nightingale Conant.

Index

978-0-595-45095-4
0-595-45095-4